D0520699

EXTRAORDINARY RECIPES FROM

FAIRFIELD COUNTY CHEF'S TABLE

AMY KUNDRAT

Photography by Stephanie Webster

CONNECTICUT'S GOLD COAST

LYONS PRESS
Guilford, Connecticut

An imprint of Globe Pequot Press

To buy books in quantity for corporate use
or incentives, call **(800) 962-0973**
or e-mail **premiums@GlobePequot.com**.

Lyons Press is an imprint of Globe Pequot Press.

All photography by Stephanie Webster

Editor: Amy Lyons
Project Editor: Lynn Zelem
Text Design: Libby Kingsbury
Layout Artist: Nancy Freeborn

Library of Congress Cataloging-in-Publication Data is available on file.

ISBN 978-0-7627-8641-1

Printed in the United States of America

10 9 8 7 6 5 4 3 2 1

Restaurants and chefs often come and go, and menus are ever-changing. We recommend you call ahead to obtain current information before visiting any of the establishments in this book.

CONTENTS

Acknowledgments

A project like this is the result of the contributions of many. My deepest gratitude must go to the chefs, restaurateurs, farmers, and artisans of Fairfield County who gave generously of their time and talent in sharing their stories and their recipes. Thank you for opening your kitchens to us.

To my family in food—the writers of CTbites and my roving gang of fellow gourmands, Steph, Ellen, Liz, Leeanne, and Jeff—your passion for our Connecticut home and its thriving food scene keeps me constantly inspired.

To my partner in all things food, Stephanie. Thank you for your friendship, partnership, and support. Your beautiful photographs on these pages are the soul of this book.

To the fine folks at Globe Pequot Press, thanks especially Amy and Chris, for your support of this project and steadfast devotion to the art of the written word.

To my mother, Nancy. Thank you for always encouraging me to experiment, explore, and take risks both inside and outside of the kitchen.

And finally to my amazing husband and favorite dining companion Ryan, whose ceaseless support, humor, and love makes a project like this, and just about everything, worthwhile.

Introduction

Situated at New England's southwesternmost point, Fairfield County stakes a claim to some of Connecticut's most diverse terrain, an enviable proximity to New York City, and a discerning community of food lovers driving the demand for a vibrant dining scene. Fairfield County encompasses thirteen towns across 625 square miles, from a bustling exurban coastline, to its suburban center, and rural enclaves due north. Unlike New Haven and Hartford, which are the clear urban centers of their counties, Fairfield County is a decentralized region of communities and Connecticut's undisputed culinary capital.

The Gold Coast boasts some of the country's toniest neighborhoods, such as Greenwich and Southport, as well as the state's largest and most culturally diverse cities, including the historic port city of Norwalk, the corporate-minded Stamford, and the state's most populous city, Bridgeport. Upscale dining, downtown dining districts, and neighborhood bodegas are equally at home along this dense and diverse corridor. Along Fairfield County's suburban center are towns such as Ridgefield, New Canaan, and Westport, whose historic Main Streets draw farmers' markets and upscale dining districts scattered with family-friendly options. At the landlocked northern fringes lies a handful of the county's most rural towns. Quiet enclaves such as Easton, Wilton, and Newtown have large swaths of protected and undeveloped land, as well as bountiful farmland and a handful of destination farm-to-table restaurants.

Welcome
to
Southport
Beach!
Dinner Begins
@ 6ish PM

Binding these disparate towns together is a diverse bounty of both land and sea. To the south, fishermen troll the shallow waters and oyster beds of Long Island Sound. To the north, small farms, orchards, and even apiaries become increasingly frequent as you migrate from the dense southern core to the county's rural fringes. This proximity to source is a draw for chefs seeking a stronger connection to the land. The bounty and diversity of the land is cultivated by farmers and fishermen, but also celebrated by chefs and diners alike.

Exemplifying this ecosystem is an abundance of weekly farmers' markets from Old Greenwich to Danbury. These markets begin to provide a glimpse into an active network of small farms. The centrally located Westport Farmers' Market is a fitting example that showcases the area's thriving food community, with a loyal following of both chefs and home cooks who are drawn to this year-round market. On any given Thursday you'll find them side by side, angling for that week's peak produce, from spring's harbingers of fiddleheads and ramps, to late summer's organic heirloom tomatoes and fall's first crop of pumpkins. The summer market brings guest chefs, cooking competitions, and handmade artisan products drawing from ingredients that are sourced rarely more than a dozen miles away.

Although Nutmeg State pride may be strong, Fairfield County's affinity for New York, as well as its influence, is impossible to deny. Situated just north of its boroughs, many towns are thirty to sixty miles from "the City," as it's affectionately known. Informed but not defined by this proximity, many of Fairfield County's residents work, eat, and play in the Big Apple. Chefs and restaurateurs are not immune to its influence and are part of a trajectory of talent that makes its way from New York's famous dining scene to Connecticut kitchens.

Fairfield County is geographically blessed. Its land is bountiful. It boasts an enviable proximity to one of the world's culinary capitals. But its most defining characteristic has nothing to do with its longitude and latitude. It's the people who make this region remarkable—the farmers, foragers, artisans, chefs, and diners who bring it all to life. Fairfield County boasts a discerning population who recognizes and appreciates its singular landscape with an uninhibited embrace of trends in food culture and fine dining. This perfect storm—a willing audience and bounty of the land—makes it an ideal location for restaurateurs and talented chefs and who want to experiment and leave their mark.

We welcome you to explore Fairfield County as only we know how, through its people and their food, captured in profile and recipe on the following pages. These recipes, many born in a commercial kitchen, have been translated with you, the home cook in mind. The best way to learn is to experiment and explore. Happy experimenting!

FOOD CHARITIES

For an affluent region where so much is given, much is also expected. Several charities that champion the causes of the hungry have emerged to help those in need in Fairfield County and beyond.

Community Plates (165 New Canaan Avenue, Norwalk, CT 06850; 800-280-3298; communityplates.org/) is a nonprofit that launched in 2010 to help connect the surplus food from restaurants and other food sources like supermarkets to food-insecure households throughout the United States. Operating in three regions across the country, including Fairfield County, Community Plates is fueled by volunteer food runners who rescue and deliver the surplus food to the places that can make a difference in the fight against hunger, such as shelters, soup kitchens, and food pantries.

Supporting farms and making their fresh, healthy, and locally grown produce available to historically underserved communities is the mission of Wholesome Wave (855 Main Street, Suite 910, Bridgeport, CT 06604; 203-226-1112; wholesomewave.org). It operates in twenty-eight states, but it is owned and operated in Bridgeport under the leadership of CEO and president Michel Nischan, a James Beard award–winning chef behind Westport's Dressing Room restaurant (page 73).

Connecticut Food Bank (P.O. Box 8686, New Haven, CT 06531; 203-469-5000; ctfoodbank.org) provides food and resources to nearly six hundred community-based food programs including soup kitchens, food pantries, and shelters across Connecticut. With a warehouse in Bridgeport and nearby New Haven (where it is headquartered), the organization's goal is to alleviate hunger through public awareness by supplying food to its member agencies. As a result of its ambition, it is the largest source of emergency food in the state, distributing an average of thirty-three tons of food, five days a week.

109 Cheese & Wine

109 Danbury Road
Ridgefield, CT 06877
(203) 438-5757
109cheeseandwine.com
Owners: Monica and Todd Brown

Bloomy, soft-ripened, blue-veined, flowery, and peppery. Ridgefield's 109 Cheese & Wine shop is a center for the education and appreciation for artisanal cheese and wine in northern Fairfield County.

Owner and cheesemonger Monica Brown, with her husband and partner, Todd Brown, fill their intimately scaled shop with a carefully curated selection of cheeses, from a creamy Hudson Valley goat cheese to a sheep's milk cheese crafted by Benedictine monks from northern France.

Cheese's perfect partners—charcuterie and gourmet snacks such as flatbreads, terrines, and hors d'oeuvres from nearby Bernard's Restaurant (page 19)—are also stocked by 109. Seasonal luxury food items such as black and white truffles, *jamón ibérico,* and caviar come and go with availability, while low-yield producers of olive oils, vinegars, and salts are staples year-round.

Located in Ridgefield's Marketplace, a European-style collection of small food shops, 109 Cheese & Wine also boasts an intimate companion shop that sells a thoughtful collection of wine and craft beers chosen for their ability to pair well with food. Rough-hewn wooden wine shelves and riddling racks line the walls of the shop, and an old barn window visually and physically connects to the adjacent cheese shop. Its scale and materials lend a feeling of intimacy, making the experience seem like a visit to the private wine cellar of a dear friend.

Private classes and tastings hosted by owner Monica Brown marry both sides of the business, from "Beer and Cheese of the Pacific Northwest" to "Pinot Noirs and the Cheeses Who Love Them." Co-owner Todd Brown, a vintage-car enthusiast, spearheads a popular picnic-basket program, with customers ordering packaged provisions for road trips near and far, or just for an evening at Ridgefield's popular Concert in the Park series.

While the cases filled with cheeses and charcuterie and the shelves piled high with wine are certainly a draw, 109 has made their savory mark with a selection of made-to-order gourmet grilled-cheese sandwiches. The not-so-secret ingredient? Fresh seasonal ingredients, such as wild mushrooms paired with a variety of cheeses. Pop-up Grilled Cheese and Raclette evenings abound in the fall, as 109's vintage Dodge pickup truck serves grilled cheeses piled high with other provisions from its flatbed, in its dual role as host and kitchen.

The perfect platform for the shop, 109's grilled cheese sandwiches combine rich and creamy cheeses with various piquant ingredients. The Wild Mushroom Grilled Cheese, made with two cheeses and three types of sautéed wild mushrooms on a freshly baked baguette, is a case in point: It pairs ideally with a white Burgundy or a red Rhône wine.

WILD MUSHROOM GRILLED CHEESE

(SERVES 4)

½ pound hen-of-the-woods or maitake mushrooms, cleaned and stems removed

½ pound shiitake mushrooms, cleaned and stems removed

1 pound portobello mushrooms, cleaned and stems removed

2 shallots, peeled and chopped

1 tablespoon fresh thyme leaves

4 tablespoons unsalted butter, plus extra for spreading

2 tablespoons olive oil

¼ teaspoon salt

¼ teaspoon fresh cracked black pepper

8 slices sourdough bread

8 ounces raclette cheese, very thinly sliced

8 ounces Al Tavolo cheese from Arethusa Farm, grated (Arethusa Farm is located in Litchfield County and their cheese, milk, and ice cream products are available at select shops across Fairfield County, such as 109 Cheese & Wine.)

2 cups baby spinach leaves, washed

Preheat oven to 350°F.

Roughly chop the mushrooms and place on a sheet pan. Sprinkle the shallots and thyme over the mushrooms. Cut 4 tablespoons butter into small chunks and spread them evenly over the mushrooms, drizzle with olive oil, and sprinkle with salt and pepper. Roast mushrooms at 350°F for 15–18 minutes, stirring occasionally.

Lightly butter the outside of 1 piece of bread, spread 2 ounces of raclette cheese on the unbuttered side of the bread, layer with one-fourth of the mushroom mixture, then add 2 ounces of Al Tavolo cheese on top of the mushrooms, and a handful of baby spinach leaves. Place the second piece of bread on top and butter it.

Heat a seasoned cast-iron or nonstick skillet over a medium-low flame (or use a heated panini machine). Place the sandwich in the pan. Cook until the underside is golden brown and the cheese is beginning to melt, 1–3 minutes. Carefully flip the sandwich. Cook until the underside is golden brown. Remove from pan, slice at an angle, and serve.

Repeat for remaining 3 sandwiches.

ARTISAN RESTAURANT

275 OLD POST ROAD
SOUTHPORT, CT 06890
(203) 307-4222
ARTISANSOUTHPORT.COM
EXECUTIVE CHEF: FREDERIC KIEFFER
OWNERS: RICK WAHLSTEDT, CHARLES MALLORY, AND
FREDERIC KIEFFER

Nestled within the boutique Delamar Hotel in Southport, Artisan anchors a pristine new-colonial compound within one of Fairfield County's toniest enclaves. A sprawling outdoor patio and bar studded with waist-high flowering planters and nattily attired guests makes arriving for a meal at Artisan Restaurant feel less like the New England tavern it was fashioned after and more akin to an elegant private country retreat.

"We wanted Artisan to feel comfortable, as if you have been invited to enjoy a weekend in the country," says Executive Chef Frederic Kieffer, a native of Paris and resident of Fairfield County. Artisan is a collaboration between three partners: Rick

Wahlstedt, owner of L'escale (page 94) in Greenwich; Charles Mallory, founder and partner of the Greenwich Hospitality Group; and Kieffer.

Artisan is Chef Kieffer's second collaboration with Delamar Hotels. He splits his time between it and his other seasonally focused, special-occasion restaurant—L'escale restaurant in Greenwich.

A chic take on New England classics is the chosen culinary center point for Artisan's local menu—and Kieffer's year-round devotion to seasonal cooking. Small plates populate the bar and tavern menu, familiar compositions that include dry-aged beef sliders, mini lobster rolls, and a New England seafood chowder with house-made fennel oyster crackers.

Shaking off any vestige of the notion of "tavern," Artisan presents its most polished persona as one moves into the dining room. The menu continues with pub classics set with a decidedly European flourish, while remaining anchored by the bounty of the nearby Connecticut shoreline and a small network of nearby farms that Kieffer and his team draw inspiration from. Simple quality ingredients are the foundation of the dishes, such as the local striped bass or a New England–style cioppino served in a lobster broth that are some of Artisan's most popular dishes.

Scandinavian-inspired furniture and artist-painted wall murals continue the tone of minimal elegance already set with Artisan's auspicious entrance. The patio acts as a welcoming emissary, the indoor bar and tavern dining embody informal elegance, and the dining room is the most polished of its personas. This careful attention to detail in the spaces serves as an important visual cue to a theme of craftsmanship found throughout the menu.

Presenting us with his upscale French take on a classic New England dish, Chef Kieffer composes his ingredient-intensive pot roast around well-marbled beef cheeks.

ARTISAN POT ROAST

(SERVES A CROWD)

For the beef cheeks:

10 pounds beef cheeks
cooking fat for sautéing

For the bouquet garni:

½ bunch parsley
10 thyme sprigs
5 bay leaves

For the sauce:

2 cups orange juice, reduced on its own by half
1 teaspoon ground coriander
4 cloves
2 pieces orange peel
4 ounces all-purpose flour
2 cups sherry wine
6 cups red wine
5 large tomatoes
3 cups chicken stock
6 cups veal stock
Water to cover, if necessary
Salt and black pepper to taste

For the pot roast:

Beef cheeks, sliced
Pot roast sauce
1 of each color rainbow baby carrots
     (purple, red, yellow, orange)
Parsnips, cut into sticks
Salt and pepper to taste
10 tablespoons butter, divided
1 sprig fresh rosemary
1 pint brussels sprouts

For the parsnip puree:

4 parsnips
Milk and heavy cream to cover
Salt to taste

For the parsnip chips:

1 parsnip
Vegetable oil
Salt to taste

Chopped parsley for garnish

To prepare beef cheeks: Clean the beef cheeks.

Sauté the beef cheeks in your preferred fat, giving them a nice brown color. Remove them from the pans.

To prepare the bouquet garni: Wash the parsley. Then lay down half of it, and place the thyme sprigs and bay leaves in the center. Top with the remaining half of the parsley and roll it tightly to resemble a little bundle, and tie with kitchen string.

For the sauce: In a separate small saucepan, reduce the orange juice on its own by half.

To your original large sauté pan with the beef cheek renderings, add the spices, ground coriander, cloves, and orange peel, and render 1 minute. Add the flour and cook for 1 minute. Add the sherry and red wine, and reduce by half. Add the reduced orange juice, and bouquet garni.

Put the cheeks back in the pan and add the stock and tomatoes. Bring to a boil, check the seasoning, cover, and bake at 300°F for 3 hours or until tender. When cooked, delicately remove the cheeks, strain the sauce, and reduce it to consistency.

Refrigerate sauce and beef cheeks separately until prepared to be served.

For the pot roast: When the beef cheeks are cold, cut them into ⅓-inch-thick slices. Place them in a shallow pot, pour the sauce over, cover, and bake at 300°F for 45 minutes.

Peel and split the baby carrots. Peel and cut the parsnips into ¼-inch-thick sticks. Place the carrots and parsnips in an ovenproof pan, season with salt and pepper, add the butter and rosemary, and bake at 325°F until fork tender.

Quarter the brussels sprouts, season them with salt and pepper, and sauté them in butter over medium-high heat.

For the parsnip puree: Peel and chop the parsnips. Place them in a saucepan and cover with half milk and half heavy cream. Season with salt, bring to a simmer, and cook for 30 minutes or until the parsnips are soft and well cooked. Strain well and puree the parsnips.

Check the seasoning, and keep the puree hot.

For the parsnip chips: Peel the parsnip and then peel off long strips of parsnips with the same vegetable peeler. Deep fry them in vegetable oil at 325°F. When gold and crispy, remove them from the oil, drain on a paper towel, and sprinkle with salt.

To serve: For each serving, place parsnip puree in a deep plate (a pasta plate is suggested). Arrange slices of pot roast over the puree. Pour a little sauce over the meat and scatter the baby carrots, parsnips, and quartered brussels sprouts over and around it. Garnish the plate with parsnip chips and chopped parsley.

BAR SUGO

102 WALL STREET
NORWALK, CT 06854
(203) 956-7134
BARSUGO.COM
OWNER/EXECUTIVE CHEF: PASQUALE PASCARELLA

With small plates, a youthful vibe, and a chef eager to challenge expectations, Bar Sugo is an energetic take on the traditional Italian restaurant experience. Chef Pasquale "Pat" Pascarella opened Bar Sugo raring to serve the type of informal and hearty Italian food

he enjoys cooking and serving—from rustic small plates, or *cicchetti*, to homemade pastas. A 2004 alum of New York's French Culinary Institute, Chef Pascarella honed his early culinary skills in the Italian-minded kitchens of Mario Batali's Esca and Scott Conant's L'Impero before moving his talents north to Stamford's Bella Luna and Saltwater Grill, and winning the city's first Iron Chef competition in 2008. Pascarella opened his first restaurant, Cortina Pizzeria, in Norwalk, focusing on pizza as his creative outlet, piling them high with his favorite ingredients, such as smoked cheeses, short ribs, and cured meats served aloft a signature cornmeal-dusted crust.

At Bar Sugo, Pascarella has the space and freedom to cultivate his laid-back Italian dining atmosphere, starting with its decor; a red-and-white tiled floor, copper-topped bar, exposed brick, and white subway-tile walls. This informal and playful approach continues to be woven through a menu of antipasti, homemade pastas, wood-fired pizzas, and cicchetti, Bar Sugo's much-lauded specialties. Ordering solely from those small plates is the ideal way to explore the food with your own tasting menu. Ask any regular to settle on one can't-miss dish, and it would certainly be Pascarella's meatballs. Inspired by his mother's and grandmother's recipes, Pascarella riffs endlessly on them, introducing foie gras, crispy veal, and chile oil in Bar Sugo's six iterations.

Bar Sugo's recent meatballs include the following variations: "Mommy's" traditional beef meatballs prepared with tomato and Grana Padano cheese; pork meatballs with red wine, tomato sauce, and whipped ricotta; duck and foie gras; Wagyu beef with Gouda, red onion jam, and truffle oil; crispy veal with Calabrian chile aioli; and "Cortina's" beef, pork, and veal with sage.

Sugo Meatballs

(SERVES 4–6)

1 pound ground beef
¼ pound ground veal
¼ pound ground pork
¼ cup of your favorite tomato sauce, plus 1¾ cups
    for finishing
1 whole egg, beaten
1 cup panko bread crumbs
10 ounces ricotta cheese
5 tablespoons grated Parmesan cheese
1 tablespoon chopped fresh basil

Salt and pepper to taste
Olive oil, to fry

Mix all ingredients in a bowl until thoroughly combined. Roll the mixture into 2-ounce balls. Pan fry in olive oil on all sides for about 4 minutes on medium-high heat until golden brown. Finish in your favorite tomato sauce. Shave some nice Grana Padano over the top and serve.

Barcelona Wine Bar

4180 Black Rock Turnpike, Fairfield, CT 06824
63 North Main Street, South Norwalk, CT 06854
222 Summer Street, Stamford, CT 06901
18 West Putnam Avenue, Greenwich, CT 06830
155 Temple Street, New Haven, CT 06510
971 Farmington Avenue, West Hartford, CT 06107
barcelonawinebar.com
Owners: Sasa Mahr-Batuz and Andy Pforzheimer

Re-creating the flavors and energy of its namesake city, Barcelona Wine Bar first opened in Norwalk in 1996 as a thirty-five-seat wine and tapas bar. Since then it has grown into a restaurant group pioneering Spanish culinary heritage with restaurants spanning eight cities. Connecticut is home to six Barcelona restaurants, each with the ability to instantly transport diners to Spain with traditional Spanish cuisine, an ambitious wine and cocktail program, and an environment of near-constant revelry.

Each Barcelona outpost is led by a different chef but overseen by the culinary vision of owners Sasa Mahr-Batuz and Andy Pforzheimer. The partners built their business inspired by a mutual admiration for Iberian culture. A native of Argentina, Mahr-Batuz lived in Spain and Portugal for several years as a professional tennis player. He joined forces with Pforzheimer, a veteran of the restaurant industry who has spent time as a chef in France, California, and New York. Mahr-Batuz brings the creative joie de vivre while Pforzheimer packs the cerebral culinary brawn.

Charcuterie, tapas, Sunday pig roasts, wine, cocktails, and a convivial bar scene are common threads throughout the locations. The menus are anchored by a rigorous food and beverage program that benefits from annual staff trips to Spain to spot trends, educate staff, and build relationships with the individual producers who age the cheeses, cure the ham, and produce the wines that set Barcelona apart.

With nearly forty small plates, you could be tempted to explore Barcelona's extensive tapas menu with perennial favorites such as chorizo with sweet-and-sour figs finished with a balsamic-sherry glaze, grilled hanger steak in black truffle sauce, and the classic southern Spanish dish of *boquerones*, or marinated fresh anchovies. Beyond the tapas menu is a carefully curated menu of charcuterie and cheeses; and entrée-size plates where you will find grilled dishes such as the *churrasco* and fish of the day.

And of course no Spanish menu is complete without its own interpretation of paella. At Barcelona, three types are offered for two to six people at the restaurant. Barcelona's pared-down version for the home cook embraces a traditional approach to seafood paella with a focus on a hefty dose of *sofrito* and perfectly prepared rice.

SEAFOOD PAELLA

Good paella is heavy on the *sofrito* and light on saffron. Great paella is all about the rice and not about the toppings. When you make paella the first time, taste the rice at regular intervals, and don't worry about some sticking to the pan. That's the best part.

(SERVES 6)

For the paella spice:

2 teaspoons ground cumin

4 teaspoons sweet smoked paprika (pimentón de la Vera dulce)

2 teaspoons turmeric

4 teaspoons ground coriander

½ teaspoon saffron threads

For the sofrito:

1 medium red bell pepper, seeded, cored, and finely chopped

1 medium green bell pepper, seeded, cored, and finely chopped

1 Spanish onion, peeled and finely chopped

3 tablespoons extra-virgin olive oil, divided

1 tablespoon minced garlic

1 teaspoon sweet paprika

1 tablespoon tomato paste

½ cup dry white wine

For the paella:

2 cups plus 3 tablespoons unsalted fish or chicken stock

6–7 threads saffron

3 tablespoons extra-virgin olive oil

1 cup thickly sliced smoked Spanish chorizo or Marcella sausage

3 chicken thighs, bone-in skin on

1 teaspoon salt

1 teaspoon pepper

3–4 shrimp, shells on

1 tablespoon sliced or minced garlic, divided

1 cup Calasparra or bomba rice

1 teaspoon prepared paella spice (instructions on p. 14)

1 cup prepared sofrito (instructions on p. 14)

8 littleneck clams, scrubbed

10 Prince Edward Island mussels, scrubbed and rinsed

To make the paella spice: Mix the spices thoroughly in a bowl. Use right away or store in an airtight container for up to 1 month.

To make the sofrito: In a food processor fitted with a metal blade, process the bell peppers and onion until they resemble chunky applesauce.

In a saucepan set over medium heat, heat 2 tablespoons of olive oil and when hot sauté 1 tablespoon of garlic for 2 minutes or until slightly browned. Add the pureed vegetables and paprika and bring to a simmer. Stir frequently while the mixture reaches the simmering point.

Add the tomato paste and white wine and simmer for 15–20 minutes or until the liquid is reduced by half and the vegetables are tender. Cover and keep the sofrito warm until needed. If not using it right away, refrigerate in a container with a tight-fitting lid for up to 2 days.

To make the paella: Preheat the oven to 450°F.

Warm the stock in a large saucepan. Spoon the 3 tablespoons of warm stock over the saffron threads in a small bowl. Allow the saffron to "bloom," coloring the liquid and releasing its aroma (about 5 minutes). Add the saffron liquid to the remaining stock and allow 10 minutes to infuse.

Heat 1 tablespoon of extra-virgin olive oil in a paella pan over medium heat. Add the chorizo and cook for 2–3 minutes, or until the fat is rendered and the sausage is slightly browned. Remove the chorizo to a clean plate and reserve.

Season the chicken with 1 teaspoon salt and 1 teaspoon pepper and sauté for 5 minutes or until lightly browned on all sides. Add the shrimp to the pan and cook until the shells begin to turn red. Remove the shrimp to a clean plate and reserve.

Return the chorizo to the pan with 1 tablespoon of garlic and cook until the garlic is fragrant. Add the rice, stir well, and sauté for 2–3 minutes. Add the paella spice and the sofrito and continue to cook for 4–5 minutes. Add the saffron-flavored stock and bring to a boil over high heat. Taste the liquid and adjust the seasoning as needed, being sure to under season the liquid slightly as the shellfish will release some brine while they cook.

Add the clams to the pan. Cover with aluminum foil and transfer the paella pan to the oven. Cook for 15 minutes and then remove the foil.

Add the shrimp and mussels to the pan. Cook for 10–15 minutes longer.

Drizzle the paella with extra-virgin olive oil and serve.

WHITE NEGRONI

(SERVES 1 COCKTAIL)

½ ounce gin (preferably Martin Miller's Gin)
1 ounce bitters (preferably Gran Classico Bitter)
1 ounce white vermouth (preferably Cocchi
    Americano Vermouth)
Lemon peel for garnish

Measure all ingredients into a clean pint-size glass. Add ice to the top, and stir until the ice melts down 25–30 percent.

Strain into small martini glass. Garnish with lemon peel.

BARTACO

Sasa Mahr-Batuz and Andy Pforzheimer's talent as Spanish restaurateurs extends south of the border to their newest concept, bartaco. Based loosely on Mexican street food, bartaco's menu is broken up into tacos, not tacos, and sides, with equal amounts of attention given over to their signature made-to-order margaritas, Latin-inspired cocktails, and a hefty list of tequilas. The atmosphere at their Stamford, Westport, West Hartford, and Port Chester, New York, outposts is upscale surfer chic, with a lively late night scene. Locations: 222 Summer Street, Stamford, CT 06901; 20 Wilton Road, Westport, CT 06880; 971 Farmington Avenue, West Hartford, CT 06107; 1 Willett Avenue, Port Chester, NY 10573; bartaco.com.

BEREKET

2871 FAIRFIELD AVENUE
BRIDGEPORT, CT 06606
(203) 333-9393
OWNER: SELAHATTIN CINAR

Traditional and unadorned, Bridgeport's Bereket restaurant is a classic interpretation of centuries-old Turkish cuisine. For a culture that celebrates home cooking and marks time by empires, the Bereket experience is an accordingly relaxed and traditional one. Owner Selahattin Cinar sees to this consistency by mining traditional halal family recipes, in keeping with the Muslim dietary law.

Bereket's first location was tucked inside the rear of a Citgo station with a lone folding table and limited to take-out orders and regulars who stood as they sipped cups of Turkish tea or coffee. Its current location on Bridgeport's Fairfield Avenue if a far cry from those inauspicious beginnings, having successfully transformed itself into a family-

friendly restaurant with tiled floors, ample seating, and white tablecloths. Although the restaurant is BYOB, a tall bar along one wall of the restaurant doubles as the restaurant's hub, frequented by regulars eating lunch, lingering over tea, or grabbing takeout.

The natural cadence of most meals at Bereket commences with a variety of simply prepared hot or cold meze, such as falafel, hummus served with warm pita bread or kofte, gently spiced lamb meatballs. Lunch and dinner revolve around lamb, beef, and chicken kebabs that can be ordered as a sandwich or a plate, served with a generous pile of rice—common in Turkish dining. Digging into less familiar territory is rewarded. A structural feat and rarity on menus, the *manti* is a dish prepared once a week by a Turkish woman who devotes her time to wrapping bits of dough around minuscule pieces of boiled lamb, which are then cooked and finished in a yogurt-based sauce seasoned with sumac.

No meal at Bereket is complete without a strong cup of Turkish coffee or Turkish tea paired with dessert. Many Turkish desserts are sweetly centered around honey, such as baklava, with its syrupy, dense layers of phyllo and chopped pistachios, or the *sütlaç,* rice pudding baked inside a clay pot. Turkish coffee at Bereket is prepared traditionally with finely ground coffee, boiled in a *cezve* with sugar and served in a small cup slightly larger than the size of a demitasse, where the grounds are allowed to settle into a dark pile at the bottom of your cup.

The *sigara borek,* a warm meze of fried papery-thin layers of phyllo dough wrapped around parsley-laced feta, is a customer favorite.

Sigara Borek

(SERVES 4)

½ cup feta cheese
⅓ cup chopped fresh parsley
1 egg (optional)

3 sheets borek pastry or phyllo dough
Oil for frying

Combine the first three ingredients in a bowl.

Roll out defrosted dough and cut into squares.

Place about 1 tablespoon of this filling on a square piece of pastry. Roll it up like a cigar. Using your finger, seal the edges of the pastry with a little water.

Fry in oil until golden brown, about 3 minutes. Let drain on a paper towel and serve garnished with a pinch of fresh parsley.

Beekeeper and honey sommelier Marina Marchese and her army of Italian honeybees are happy to call Weston home. As founder of Red Bee Apiary (866-530-3022; redbee.com), Marchese presides over sixteen hives, each filled with about sixty thousand bees that power an artisanal line of honeys and honey-based products. Do the math: That makes an army of 960,000 bees at her disposal—nearly the entire population of Fairfield County.

Like wine, honey is dependent on terroir for flavor; the source of the flowering plants that the honeybee visits for nectar imparts its distinctive flavor and provides a breadth of complexity, color, and texture. Red Bee's honeys, named for such influencers as alfalfa, buckwheat, and tulip poplar, are intrinsically linked to the Connecticut landscape. *The Accidental Beekeeper* is an apt title for Marchese's first book, part memoir and part history of beekeeping. Marchese was smitten with bees after visiting a neighbor's backyard hive, which inspired her to jettison her career as a designer for a life filled with bees. Today Red Bee honey is a highly coveted product served in Fairfield County's best eateries and at some of the best food shops in New York City, such as Murray's Cheese Shop and Eataly.

Marchese is the founder of the American Honey Tasting Society and president of the Backyard Beekeepers Association in Connecticut, the country's largest beekeeping club with over five hundred members. She often lectures and leads honey tastings both at Red Bee Apiary and across the region.

BERNARD'S RESTAURANT & SARAH'S WINE BAR

20 WEST LANE (ROUTE 35)
RIDGEFIELD, CT 06877
(203) 438-8282
BERNARDSRIDGEFIELD.COM
OWNERS/CHEFS: BERNARD AND SARAH BOUISSOU

Like the town's quaint Main Street and its iconic Cass Gilbert–designed marble fountain, Bernard's Restaurant is an essential part of Ridgefield's town vernacular. It would be impossible to imagine this historic town without this charming French restaurant and its equally charismatic owners/chefs Bernard and Sarah Bouissou. The ninth of ten children growing up in southern France, Bernard made his way to New York City and worked inside some of its most venerable French kitchens, including Plaza Athenée and Le Cirque with Daniel Boulud, as well as Le Cygne and La Panetière. Along the way—literally "on the line" at Le Cirque—he met Sarah, a fellow chef and veteran of Thomas Keller's Rakel. They soon married, merged their talents, and made their way out to the suburbs to call Ridgefield home to both family and a restaurant.

A master of classical French techniques, Bernard makes rich, complicated dishes appear effortless. The menu changes daily and often features his signature tuna tartare napoleon, a bouillabaisse, and foie gras trio served smoked, au torchon, and sautéed. The more formal restaurant, with its equally formal menu, occupies a series of well-appointed downstairs dining rooms and a patio in a flowering outdoor garden. Serving as exterior dining spaces, the gardens are home to wine dinners and private events en plein air when the weather allows, making Bernard's synonymous with special occasions and destination dining in northern Fairfield County.

A commanding yet disarming presence, Bernard rules the kitchen while the tireless Sarah ensures the smooth running of its dining rooms and the upstairs eatery, Sarah's Wine Bar. The cozy complement to Bernard's more formal presentation, the wine bar is a

relaxed bar and lounge with a menu that skews more informal bistro but shares a kitchen and hits the same French-influenced notes. Wines by the glass and small plates are encouraged, and live music and a roaring fire are frequent dining companions.

With a reputation as one of Fairfield County's finest traditional French eateries, the actual experience of both Bernard's and Sarah's is a much more soulful family affair, favoring warmth and hospitality over buttoned-up Gallic formality.

Embodying both sides of the Bouissous, Bernard's contemporary presentation of crispy sweetbreads embraces classical French flavors.

CRISPY SWEETBREADS WITH BUTTERNUT SQUASH, HARICOTS VERTS, FRISÉE & CHANTERELLE SALAD WITH SHERRY SHALLOT VINAIGRETTE

(SERVES 6)

For the sherry shallot vinaigrette (makes 9.5 ounces):

1 tablespoon Dijon mustard
1 tablespoon sherry vinegar
1 tablespoon hot water
1 cup blend of canola and olive oil
1 shallot, peeled and chopped fine
Salt and pepper to taste

For the salad:

2 pounds sweetbreads (after cleaning this should
    yield about 1¼ pounds)
¼ pound haricots verts
Salt to taste
1 head frisée
1 butternut squash
¼ pound chanterelles, cleaned and sliced
1 tablespoon olive oil
2 tablespoons vegetable oil
2 tablespoons unsalted butter
2 tablespoons fresh sage, minced
Pepper to taste
2 tablespoons chopped fresh chives

To make the vinaigrette: In a bowl whisk together mustard, vinegar, and hot water, slowly drizzle in the blended oil, and add chopped shallots. Salt and pepper to taste.

To prepare salad: Clean the sweetbreads. Separate them into sections and remove the membrane. Cut them into 1-inch pieces.

Blanch the haricots verts in salted water for about 4 minutes until tender. Drain and chill in ice water (this stops the cooking). When cooled, drain and set aside.

Clean the frisée and cut it into small pieces.

Peel butternut squash and cut the top neck into 6 slices about ⅛-inch thick; set aside. Remove the seeds from the round end and julienne the remaining squash. Sauté all of the squash in olive oil for about 2 minutes until tender but not overcooked. Remove from pan, cool, and set aside.

Using a preheated hot grill or grill pan, brush the butternut squash slices with olive oil and grill for 2–3 minutes, making crosshatch marks before turning over. Set aside.

In a bowl combine the frisée, haricots verts, and julienned butternut squash.

Preheat a medium-size cast iron skillet to medium-high heat, add 2 tablespoons vegetable oil, and place the seasoned sweetbreads in the bottom of the pan—do not overlap the pieces.

Caramelize the sweetbreads on both sides, giving them a nice golden color.

Sauté chanterelles in oil then add butter and sage.

Season the salad of frisée, haricots verts, butternut squash, and chopped chives with salt and pepper and toss with vinaigrette.

In the center of the plate, place the grilled butternut squash, top with the salad (using a metal ring helps hold everything in place and makes for a nice presentation), and divide and distribute the sweetbreads and chanterelles evenly around each plate.

Remove the optional metal rings and serve.

Bobby Q's / Bar Q

42 Main Street
Westport, CT 06880
(203) 454-7800
bobbyqsrestaurant.com

261 Main Street
Stamford, CT 06901
(203) 316-0278
barqstamford.com
Owner: Bobby Q. LeRose

Is there such a thing as Connecticut barbecue? When your culinary craft is a culture dominated by big states such as Texas, how can a northern interloper possibly compete?

Bobby Q's BBQ & Grill of Westport has been challenging that notion daily since opening in the heart of Westport in 2004, serving barbecue's acolytes and newcomers alike. In its early years, many locals relied on the restaurant for indoctrination to barbecue's language of wood, charcoal, cuts of meat, smoke, and seasoning. But fast-forward a few years, and you have one of Connecticut's most eminent examples of barbecue north of the Mason-Dixon Line, as well as one of its staunchest ambassadors.

"We seek to demystify barbecue. Bobby Q's is about being respectful to traditional barbecue. We are not necessarily southern-style or Kansas City or Texas. We developed our own recipes and eventually our own style," explains owner and barbecue enthusiast Bobby LeRose.

LeRose's passion for barbecue was first ignited by a trip to Kansas City, a town where barbecue is a way of life. Back home in Connecticut, investing in and experimenting with his own pit smoker soon set him on a path that led him to open his own family-friendly barbecue restaurant that embraces a style he describes as "straight down the middle."

As Bobby Q's proves, there is more to Kansas City–, Memphis-, or Texas-style barbecue than geographic happenstance. It's truly about the details, from the type of wood that imparts that all-important smoky flavor, to the cuts and quality of meat, and the presence or lack thereof of rubs, spices, and finishing sauces. LeRose has embraced the latter into an award-winning line of Bobby Q's barbecue sauces and rubs that are sold nationwide. Libations figure prominently in the Bobby Q formula, with beer and bourbon given special attention as appropriate foils for the robust flavors of his smoke-centric menus.

In addition to the original Westport location, a newer Stamford outpost, Bar Q, opened in 2012. This trendier progeny takes the same concepts that made Bobby Q's a destination, and skews them toward the younger, more urban Stamford, with smaller plates and "snacks," a drink menu that rivals the depth of the accompanying barbecue menu, and a lively loft interior that draws younger crowds.

Perhaps the most significant of Bobby Q's roles is self-appointed. LeRose is an ambassador of barbecue. His focus on education has become intrinsically tied to his business. Through continued education classes, guest pit-master appearances, festival and events, and, most notably for Fairfield County residents, the annual Blues, Views & BBQ Festival in Westport, LeRose has undoubtedly given Connecticut its own stake in the world of barbecue.

BLUES, VIEWS & BBQ FESTIVAL

The Blues, Views & BBQ Festival is the largest backyard barbecue competition on the East Coast. Celebrating its sixth anniversary in 2013, the festival has grown to attract five thousand people each day; the two-day festival draws fans of barbecue, music, and family revelry from across Fairfield County and beyond. The event is hosted by Westport Downtown Merchants Association, and was first conceived by Bobby LeRose, who hosts both a kid's competition as well as an amateur competition with Kansas City Barbeque Society judges. Visit bluesviewsbbq.com.

BRISKET & BEEF BURNT ENDS

(SERVES 8)

1 (8–12 pound) brisket with a nice "fat cap" on top
(avoid brisket flats or "nose-off" briskets)
1 bottle Bobby Q's All-Purpose Rub

1 bag hickory wood chips, soaked (for grill/smoker)
1 cup apple juice in a spray bottle

Thoroughly rub the brisket with Bobby Q's All-Purpose Rub. Let the meat sit for at least 30 minutes or overnight. Plan for about 1½ hours per pound to cook brisket. The smoke ring, that pink color that forms beneath the surface of the brisket, is formed only while the meat is below 140°F.

Place soaked wood chips directly on charcoal or create a chip poach for a gas grill by placing the chips in aluminum foil and folding the edges to create a pouch. Poke holes in the pouch to allow the smoke to escape and place the pouch directly on the gas grill's flavor grates. It is also recommended to add a pan of water directly under area you will place meat. (Note: You must create indirect heat.) Light or ignite one side of the grill and place the meat, fat side up, on the opposite cooking grate and over the water pan. The smoker or grill should be 225°F–250°F.

I prefer to place brisket closest to heat source for at least first hour of cooking. Let brisket cook at least 1½ hours before spraying with apple juice to add flavor and keep the meat moist. If you baste too soon, the rub won't have a chance to set up on the surface of the meat and you'll end up washing away much of it. Continue basting every hour and adding wood chips for a steady stream of smoke.

Cook the brisket until the internal temperature reaches 165°F. Remove the brisket from the smoker/grill and wrap it tightly in foil. Return to the smoker/grill and continue cooking at 200°F–250°F until tender or to an internal temperature of 185°F–190°F.

Remove the meat from the smoker and let stand for 10–30 minutes. Remove foil and slice off the brisket's cap portion; reserve the flat portion to serve later. The cap portion will become the burnt ends. Trim excess fat from the cap and cut the cap into cubes. Thoroughly rub cubes of brisket with more Bobby Q's All-Purpose Rub. Place it back on grill/smoker at 250°F for an additional 2–4 hours until tender and succulent. Slice the flat portion of brisket and serve burnt ends with barbecue sauce (preferably one of Bobby Q's award-winning Nice Rack BBQ sauces).

PIT BEANS

(SERVES 8)

32 ounces of your favorite brand of canned
baked beans
⅓ cup Bobby Q's Nice Rack House Original
BBQ Sauce
½ cup chopped cooked barbecue
2 tablespoons molasses
¼ cup light brown sugar

Hickory chips, soaked (for grill/smoker)

Combine all ingredients and adjust molasses, brown sugar, and barbecue sauce to taste. Place on grill/smoker and smoke for 30 minutes. Remove from the smoker and cook over medium-low heat for 15 minutes.

BODEGA TACO BAR

1700 POST ROAD
FAIRFIELD, CT 06824
(203) 292-9590

980 POST ROAD
DARIEN, CT 06820
(203) 655-8500
BODEGATACOBAR.COM
OWNER/CHEF: MICHAEL YOUNG

Bodega Taco Bar may rival the intimate scale of a bodega, but this hip sliver of a space with its inspired Mexican street food and cozy bar serving a formidable list of tequilas is anything but modest. Chef and owner Michael Young, who first made his mark in Fairfield County with the Venezuelan-inspired Valencia Luncheria (page 178) in Norwalk, joined forces with Luis Chavez and Mario Fontana to craft a brash menu that embraces the Americas, from South America to North America, settling most centrally on Mexico.

Antojitos or "little cravings" set the tone for a menu inspired by Mexican street food that borrows frequently from abroad. House favorites such as the hoisin-glazed pork-belly *arepa*, a play on the classic Asian dish centered around richly flavored pork and surrounded by a fresh corn cake, kicks off this Latin-meets-the-world cuisine. Moving

through the menu's *platos, ensaladas,* and *tortas,* and on to the all-important tacos, the team at Bodega embraces a geographical spectrum of taco inspiration. From Baja (a panko-crusted mahimahi, pico de gallo, lemon aioli) to Korea (a crispy Korean chicken with red pepper paste and Asian slaw) and back to Mexico (with a carne asada), all of Bodega's tacos are tucked between two corn tortilla shells. Ingredients may skip across the continents, but they always return to Mexico; a perfect example is the grilled corn with cotija cheese, lime, and ancho-chile dust, a traditional street food that is in constant rotation.

Bodega also takes its tequila seriously, with deep offerings of various *blanco* ("white" or silver), *reposado* ("rested"), and *anejos* ("aged"), as well as a few mescals, topping out around fifty different selections. The agave worship extends to a selection of cocktails, or *bebidas,* that also leverage the spirit. If you're not a fan, there is also a small selection of appropriately named "not tequilas."

Family-friendly in the early evenings, Bodega's bar scene thickens and the din increases accordingly as night falls. Bodega's outsize personality makes up for its tiny footprint, and its influence has recently extended it to a second, slightly larger location in Darien.

The ultimate comfort food with a kick, the Camarones "Enchilados" is a textural tour de force that features spicy shrimp nestled in creamy *arroz con crema mexicana* and crisp mango-jicama salad.

CAMARONES "ENCHILADOS"

(SERVES 4)

For the rice:

¼ cup small-diced white onion
¼ cup diced red peppers
¼ cup diced carrots
¼ cup green peas
1 tablespoon olive oil
3 cups cooked white rice
¼ cup cotija cheese
¼ cup heavy cream
4 tablespoons unsalted butter
Salt and pepper to taste

For the tomato sauce:

1 large white onion, diced
3 cloves garlic, minced
¼ cup olive oil
13 whole dried chiles de árbol, stemmed
1 tablespoon Mexican oregano
1 (5-ounce) can tomato paste
1 (28-ounce) can whole plum tomatoes
Salt and pepper to taste

For the shrimp:

1½ pounds shrimp, cleaned and deveined,
    with tails on
2 tablespoons ancho chile powder
Salt and pepper to taste
2 tablespoons olive oil

For the salad:

¼ cup julienned mango
¼ cup julienned jicama
¼ cup julienned red pepper
2 tablespoons olive oil
½ tablespoon lime juice
9 pieces of cilantro chopped 2 inches long

To make the rice: Sauté all vegetables in olive oil for 2 minutes. Add rice. When rice is incorporated with vegetables, add cheese, heavy cream, and butter until mixed and incorporated. Season with salt and pepper to taste.

To make the sauce: Sauté onions and garlic in olive oil until onions are translucent. Add chiles de árbol and sauté for a minute. Add oregano and tomato paste. Cook for 2 minutes, then add can of plum tomatoes. Lower temperature to simmer and cook for 1 hour. Let tomatoes cool, then puree. Add salt and pepper to taste.

To prepare the shrimp: Coat the shrimp with the chile powder, and season them with salt and pepper. Sauté in hot skillet with olive oil for 3 minutes on each side, then add the prepared tomato sauce to shrimp.

To make the salad: Toss the ingredients for the salad.

To assemble: Place rice in the center of a serving platter. Spoon sauce over shrimp, but do not completely cover rice. Place salad on top of shrimp and rice and serve.

Tacos

Fairfield County's devotion to the taco extends to both ends of the dining spectrum, from trendy spots in the suburbs such as Bodega Taco Bar (page 26), to the trucks and bodegas in the cities, such as El Charrito in Stamford and Los Portales in Norwalk.

Most taco joints are city-centric, with Norwalk and Stamford staking claim to some of Fairfield County's best tacos. Norwalk is home to Los Molcajetes (211 Liberty Square; 203-831-9921), Tacos Mexico (82 Fort Point Street; 203-866-6256; tacosmexicollc.com), and Los Portales (49 Fort Point Street; 203-854-9283), taquerias that offer traditional tacos such as *carnita, lengua,* and *chicharrón,* wrapped in two corn tortillas and garnished with chopped onion, fresh cilantro, and a lime wedge.

Stamford's most notable tacos are found at Casa Villa (page 48), a taqueria that recently upgraded to a full-blown restaurant, and the truck-bound tacos of El Charrito (elcharritollc.com; truck located in front of Beamer's Café and Triple J on Richmond Hill Avenue).

Just north and east, respectively, of these are Pancho's Tacos in Danbury (145 White Street; panchostaco.com) and Taqueria La Michoacana in Bridgeport (1914 Main Street; 203-572-0004), the taco capitals of their towns.

Other relative newcomers are a pair of bartaco (page 15) restaurants in Stamford and Westport as well as Bodega, located in Fairfield and Darien. These hot spots celebrate the taco, but you'll pay for the location.

BONDA RESTAURANT

75 HILLSIDE ROAD
FAIRFIELD, CT 06824
(203) 292-9555
BONDARESTAURANT.COM
OWNER/CHEF: JAMIE COOPER

It's difficult to imagine any other restaurant fitting into its neighborhood quite as well as Bonda. Chef and owner Jamie Cooper, a constant presence inside Bonda's dining room and kitchen, is a friendly fixture in this Greenfield Hills neighborhood of Fairfield.

A native of Fairfield, Cooper's love of cooking is rivaled only by his equally voracious curiosity for wine. With no formal training and little commercial experience, he fused these passions into a lucrative catering business, running Abbondanza in Westport from 2001 to 2010 with regular appearances at Greenwich and Nantucket food and wine festivals. His fans followed him north as he naturally transitioned from caterer to restaurateur in 2010. Bonda's fixed location allows him the focus and control that has elevated Cooper and the restaurant into Fairfield County's beloved preppy American chef and bistro.

Inside Bonda, Cooper can be found routinely greeting customers both familiar and new, recommending dishes, and always pouring wine. Designed by Jamie and his wife, Kim, both the restaurant's bar area and dining room manage to feel both upscale and polished yet unpretentious—just like the Coopers. The walls are bathed in a rich orange hue and adorned with large vintage French posters; there are dark wood floors and white trim accents. A welcoming bistro-like space with about sixty seats, Bonda is the culinary soul for this largely suburban neighborhood, just north of the well-beaten path of downtown Fairfield.

Although many think of Bonda as a special occasion place, it is clear that most of its regular customers think of it affectionately as their friendly neighborhood "joint." The Bonda menu has classic American backbone with familiar glimpses of a Mediterranean Abbondanza past in its short list of appetizers and entrees that changes every few weeks. But like any true neighborhood spot, there are a few dishes on the menu that dare not leave print. One of these, the grilled romaine salad has a cultlike following, thanks to a perfect marriage of a charred and crunchy head of romaine dressed with parsley-caper vinaigrette and finished with a cascade of Grana Padano cheese. And like any bistro worthy of its category, Bonda makes a mean burger. Their individual take is a beef patty served on a toasted English muffin with caramelized onions, cheddar, and aioli.

Also known for his fish dishes, Cooper embraces the sea but keeps his attention on the details with layers of texturally interesting vegetables and bright sauces. This pan-roasted Arctic char is served with a medley of crushed potatoes, artichoke hearts, and arugula joined by a tangy pesto.

PAN ROASTED ARCTIC CHAR OVER CRUSHED POTATOES, ARTICHOKE HEARTS & ARUGULA WITH OVEN-ROASTED TOMATO-ALMOND PESTO & PRESERVED LEMON

(SERVES 4)

For the potatoes:

12 baby Yukon gold potatoes, skin on
Salt to taste
Canola oil for frying

For the artichokes:

6 very good–quality marinated whole long-stem
    artichokes, cut in half lengthwise
Extra-virgin olive oil for sautéing

For the tomato-almond pesto:

¼ cup almonds, toasted
5–6 plum tomatoes, roasted and skins removed
6 cloves roasted garlic
⅓ cup extra-virgin olive oil
Salt and pepper to taste

For the Arctic char:

4 (6-ounce) Arctic char fillets, with skin on
Salt and pepper to taste
Extra-virgin olive oil for cooking

1 bunch arugula, cleaned and left whole
4 teaspoons preserved lemon, chopped
Extra virgin olive oil for garnish

Prepare the potatoes: Boil the potatoes in generously salted water until tender. Drain. Once cool, place potatoes (one by one) in the palm of your hand and flatten the potato with your other palm. Meanwhile, heat ¼ inch of canola oil in a fry pan. When the oil is hot, fry the potatoes on both sides until golden brown and crispy, about 2–3 minutes per side. Fry the potatoes in batches, and set them on a roasting pan. Potatoes can be prepared a couple hours ahead.

Prepare the artichoke hearts: Heat a large sauté pan until hot. Add some extra-virgin olive oil and place the artichoke hearts in the pan, cut side down, for 2–3 minutes. Sauté artichoke hearts (in batches) until the cut side is golden brown. Set aside on the roasting pan with potatoes. Artichoke hearts can be prepared a couple hours ahead.

Prepare the tomato-almond pesto: Hand chop the toasted almonds so that they are coarse and don't become pasty. In a food processor, combine the tomatoes, roasted garlic cloves, and extra-virgin olive oil and process until smooth. Transfer to a bowl and stir in the chopped almonds by hand. Season to taste with salt and pepper. The pesto can be prepared hours ahead. You will have extra, and it will last in the fridge for about a week.

To finish the dish: Preheat your oven to 350°F. Season the Arctic char with salt and pepper. Heat an ovenproof sauté pan over a high flame so that the pan is very hot. Add extra-virgin olive oil to pan and place fish, skin side down, in pan. Cook char for 1–2 minutes, until the skin has become crispy. Turn the fish over and place the pan in the oven for 6–8 minutes. Reheat potatoes and artichokes in the oven while the fish is roasting.

To serve: Place 2–3 tablespoons of tomato-almond pesto on each plate. Top the pesto first with 3 crushed potatoes, then a small handful of arugula, and then 3 artichoke heart halves. Place the char, skin side down, on top and garnish with preserved lemon and extra-virgin olive oil.

Boxcar Cantina

44 Old Field Point Road
Greenwich, CT 06830
(203) 661-4774
BOXCARCANTINA.COM
Owner/Chef: Nancy Roper

Inspired by the cantinas of New Mexico and its home in Connecticut, Boxcar Cantina in Greenwich is a southwestern respite most deeply rooted in the soil of Fairfield County.

Locally sourced and organic ingredients have continued to be a signature of Boxcar's New Mexican–inspired menu since its inception nearly twenty years ago. Behind this continued success (a second restaurant opened just over the border in Bedford, New York, in 2012) is owner and chef Nancy Allen Roper, who was raised in Albuquerque, just five miles north of Route 66. This cultural provenance is directly reflected in the restaurant, from its dusty adobe-colored tile floor and walls decorated with midcentury

Americana, to its menu bursting with chiles, tacos, and margaritas. Its kitchen, an actual boxcar, bestowed the restaurant's name and gave it its spiritual and culinary hub.

Boxcar Cantina's consistent weekly presence at the Westport Farmers' Market is a way to stay up close and personal with farm-fresh ingredients, inspiring a rotation of seasonal tamales, and is an important source for nurturing relationships with the farmers who grow much of the restaurant's produce. This dedication to seasonality and a focus on sustainability on-premise has netted them one of the state's first green restaurant certifications.

Boxcar Cantina embraces is its own take on cantina cooking, resulting in what one could characterize as southwestern farm-centric cuisine with a green conscious. Organic Rancho Gordo beans, seasonal vegetables, and local grass-fed beef (some sourced from nearby Bridgewater, Connecticut) serve as the foundation for the restaurant's popular dishes, including enchiladas, tacos, burritos, and the crowd-pleasing Cowboy Burger.

I know no better place to start on Boxcar's menu than with a margarita and a bowl of guacamole. Boxcar's gently mashed version is creamy yet still chunky, with large shards of discernible avocado. The house margarita, a combination of Cuervo Tradicional, fresh-squeezed lime juice, and triple sec, begs endless iterations and experimentation: frozen, on the rocks, fruit, salt, or no salt.

BOXCAR GUACAMOLE

(SERVES 2–4)

2 ripe avocados

Juice of ½ lime

1 scallion, chopped, using both the green and white portions

1 clove garlic, peeled and chopped

¼ cup chopped fresh cilantro

Dash of hot sauce (Boxcar uses a house-made, secret-recipe hot sauce called Mucho Macho, but Cholula is also recommended; optional)

Generous pinch of Maldon sea salt

Carefully slice each avocado lengthwise around its circumference and remove the large pit. Crosshatch the avocado fruit and scoop it into a nonreactive bowl. Add the lime juice, scallion, garlic, cilantro, and hot sauce. With a fork or knife, mix the avocado; the more you mix the smoother the guacamole becomes. At Boxcar Cantina, chunky guacamole rules. Add a generous pinch of Maldon sea salt, mix again; taste again, adding more salt if desired.

Boxcar "Super Chief" Margarita

THE PERFECT MARGARITA

(MAKES 1 MARGARITA SERVED IN A 10-OUNCE GLASS)

Ice

2 ounces lime juice

½ ounce orange juice (fresh squeezed is best)

½ teaspoon organic cane sugar

4 ounces 100 percent agave tequila (see Note)

1½ ounces triple sec

Salt for the rim (optional)

Wedge of lime for garnish

Fill a glass to the brim with ice. Pour the measured ice along with all the margarita ingredients (except the salt) into a martini shaker and shake until it is cool to the touch. Salt the rim of the glass before pouring in margarita, if desired. Garnish with a lime wedge.

Note: Boxcar Cantina uses Jose Cuervo Tradicional, a *reposado*-style tequila. *Reposado* means the tequila has been aged or "rested" in oak barrels a minimum of 2 months, but less than 1 year. This process gives the tequila a slightly smoother, more complex flavor compared to blanco-style tequila, which has not been aged and is stored in stainless steel or neutral oak barrels. Either style of tequila is acceptable for a great margarita. But one thing is for certain: Do not bother with anything less than 100 percent agave tequila, or you will regret it!

SOUTHWEST CHOPPED SALAD

This simple, hearty salad is a great meal by itself or as a complement to grilled meats year-round. It is dressed with a classic French Dijon vinaigrette where good-quality Dijon mustard is the most important ingredient.

(SERVES 2–4)

For the balsamic vinaigrette dressing:

1½ teaspoons Dijon mustard
1 tablespoon balsamic vinegar
2 tablespoons extra-virgin olive oil
Squeeze of lemon juice
Dash of Maldon sea salt

For the salad:

1 organic heart of romaine or locally grown lettuce of
    your choice (one of Boxcar Cantina's favorite lettuce
    varieties is called Breen and comes from Riverbank
    Farm in Roxbury, Connecticut)
½ cup black beans
½ cup pinto beans
2 tomatoes, sliced in half, seeded, and cut into small
    cubes, about ½ cup (Tomatoes in season are best;
    use organic plum tomatoes out of season. NEVER
    refrigerate tomatoes!)
2 scallions, chopped (use white and green parts),
    or 2 tablespoons finely chopped Bermuda onion
½ cup small-cubed local, artisanal cheese (Boxcar likes
    Sankow Farm's Pleasant Cow cheese or Beltane
    Farm's goat feta; it's fun to experiment.)
1 ripe avocado, peeled, seeded, and cubed

To make the dressing: In a small bowl, whisk together the Dijon mustard, lemon juice, salt, and balsamic vinegar. Create a thick emulsion by slowly pouring in the extra-virgin olive oil, whisking constantly.

To assemble the salad: Wash lettuce leaves carefully to save all inner "baby" leaves, which look nice left whole. Spin the lettuce dry and tear it into bite-size pieces. In a large salad bowl combine the lettuce, black beans, pinto beans, tomatoes, scallions, cheese, and avocado. Toss with the dressing and serve.

MARKETS

A steady flow of weekly farmers' markets provides a glimpse into the robust network of small farms, markets, and artisan producers from Old Greenwich to Danbury. In addition to supplying local produce and products, these markets serve as an informal networking hub for food-industry veterans who attend as much to shop as to catch up with colleagues and farmers. There are over a dozen markets, but the weekly, year-round Westport Farmers' Market (50 Imperial Avenue, Westport, CT; westportfarmersmarket.com) is a standout example. Held Thursday, it has emerged as a center for shoppers and chefs alike, who return weekly to meet with farmers, take part in cooking demonstrations, and test out local products. Lori Cochran Douglas, the Westport market director, estimates that the market draws about thirty vendors and thousands of visitors weekly since it first launched in 2006.

FARMS

The population density that increases exponentially as one travels south in Fairfield County means most of its farms are relegated to northeastern towns such as Newtown, Easton, and Wilton. Ambler Farm in Wilton (257 Hurlbutt Street, Wilton, CT 06897; 203-834-1143; amblerfarm.org), a twenty-two-acre, two-hundred-year-old working farm and seasonal farm stand, has one of the most robust year-round educational programs. An important community resource for the town of Wilton, Ambler Farm's historic outbuildings serve as a tangible link to the town's, and the region's, agrarian past. Millstone Farms master farmer Annie Farrel, is a well-respected figure and frequent host of farm programs on topics such as pickling, canning, and "How to Raise Backyard Chickens."

Relatively young organic farms such as Shortt's in Sandy Hook (52 Riverside Road, Sandy Hook, CT; 203-426-9283; shorttsfarmandgarden.com), Sport Hill Farm in Easton (596 Sport Hill Road, Easton, CT; 203-268-3137; sporthillfarm.com), and Holbrook Farm & Market in Bethel (45 Turkey Plain Road, Bethel, CT; 203-792-0561; holbrookfarm.net) hug the northern fringes of Fairfield County. Shortt's is known for their diverse organic produce, and Sport Hill Farm's Patti Popp is a frequent collaborator for lower Fairfield County's dining scene.

Holbrook Farm is the "retirement project" for couple John and Lynn Holbrook, whose 13-acre farm supports a handful of northern Fairfield County restaurants such as Stanziato's (page 152) and La Zingara (page 99) as well as its neighbors in Bethel and Redding.

FARM DINNERS

Wakeman Town Farm in Westport (134 Cross Highway, Westport, CT; wakemantownfarm.org) and Millstone Farm in Wilton (180 Millstone Road, Wilton CT 06897; millstonefarm.org) are frequent protagonists of the region's farm dining scene, collaborating frequently with chefs such as Tim LaBant from The Schoolhouse at Cannondale (page 135) to host informal en plein air dinners—a popular summer ritual across Fairfield County.

BURGERS, SHAKES & FRIES

800 POST ROAD
DARIEN, CT 06820
(203) 202-9401

302 DELAVAN AVENUE
GREENWICH, CT 06830
(203) 531-7433
BURGERSSHAKESNFRIES.COM
OWNER/CHEF: KORY WOLLINS

You will not meet anyone more passionate or protective of the burger in Fairfield County than Kory Wollins. Synonymous with the trifecta of Burgers, Shakes & Fries, Wollins's mastery of this American classic helped to usher the burgeoning boutique burger trend into Connecticut.

Wollins began his first solo business venture with a challenge to himself: "What is the best product I can provide my customers for under ten dollars, and what can I make the most simply, with the best quality?" That question led the Cornell grad, with many years of restaurant-management experience, to tackle one of our country's most iconic foods: the burger.

Burgers, Shakes & Fries opened in the Greenwich neighborhood of Byram in 2007 and expanded to Darien in 2010. The original BSF, as its regulars affectionately call it, occupied only three hundred square feet. The small space underscored Wollins's focus on "delivering value," a long-held business instinct that told him to keep the space small and its core products few. Focusing just on burgers, shakes, and fries was a way to control variables and minimize waste, and it allowed Wollins and his crew to focus their time and talents to craft what has become a textbook example of a great burger.

The inception of the BSF burger, from its bun to the meat, was initially iterative. Wollins first set on using a Martin's potato roll, but the flavor of the cooked burger patty and its ratio of bread to meat wasn't quite right. On a whim, Wollins buttered toast and placed it astride his burger patty, and soon BSF's signature burger on buttered grilled toast was born. The toast is a Pullman-style loaf from nearby Rockland Bakery, but since opening his Darien location and dialing in his ground-beef ratios, the potato roll has been introduced on menu as an option to the applause of many Martin's lovers.

As for the most important burger ingredient, Wollins looks to Master Purveyors, a family-owned butcher that is a hand-cut prime house for meat. Working with Master

ensures specificity and consistency, with each BSF burger a combination of hand-cut chuck made up of 20 percent porterhouse tail and a "less course" grind. The result, according to Wollins, is "satisfyingly fatty, with just a hint of steakiness that makes the meat puff better and hold the juices better."

Fries (from sweet potato to regular fries) and shakes, the all-important companions to any burger, are not just a BSF afterthought. Starting with house-made syrups, their shakes extend from a range of traditional flavors such as vanilla, chocolate, strawberry, and coffee, to the more creative Neapolitan, black and white, and cinnamon.

BSF BURGER WITH GOOD OLD AMERICAN CHEESE

Beginning with quality ingredients and taking time to assemble your burger is the key to the BSF Burger with "good old American cheese."

(MAKES 2 BURGERS)

For the frizzled onions:

8 cups canola oil for frying
1 Vidalia onion, thinly sliced into rings no more than ⅛-inch thick
1 cup whole milk
4 cups all-purpose flour, or enough for dredging
1 tablespoon salt
1 teaspoon pepper

For the special sauce:

4 parts mayo
1 part ketchup
Various other flavor components like onion, garlic, Worcestershire sauce, hot sauce, and/or fresh herbs (basically anything you can think of)

For the burgers:

Salt and fresh ground pepper to taste
12 ounces fresh ground chuck (80/20), formed into two patties approximately ½-inch thick and 5 inches in diameter
4 slices firm white bread
4 tablespoons softened butter
4 slices best-quality American cheese (your favorite)
2 big lettuce leaves, preferably romaine or green leaf lettuce (but any lettuce will do)
4 ripe tomato slices
Thinly sliced dill pickles
2 tablespoons special sauce (see ingredients above)

To make frizzled onions: Place oil in a pot large enough so the oil is only 2–3 inches deep. Preheat it over medium heat and, using a candy thermometer, bring the temperature to 325°F.

Toss the onions in milk and separate the rings, being careful not to break the rings. Let sit for 5 minutes to neutralize the onions' acids. Meanwhile mix the flour, salt, and pepper in a large bowl.

Drain the onions in a colander and immediately add them to the bowl of seasoned flour. Toss the onions so they are all separate and evenly coated with flour. Working in small batches, drop the onions into the hot oil carefully and gently toss them with a set of metal tongs until evenly golden brown; quickly remove them from oil and let drain on a plate lined with paper towels to absorb any excess oil. Repeat until all onions are fried (Note: The oil can be cooled, strained, and reused for a few weeks. Store the cold oil, covered, in a cool, dark place.)

To make special sauce: Now I can't realistically give this recipe away as it is one of our big secrets, but you can easily come up with your own recipe by combining the ingredients. Season to taste with salt and pepper.

To assemble the burger: Preheat the broiler to low and set an oven rack as high as possible in your oven.

Salt and pepper the burger patties on one side and place them on a broiler tray in oven. (I wrap my tray with aluminum foil for easy cleanup.) Cook burgers for 4 minutes, then flip the burger and continue to cook it for another 3 minutes.

While the burger is broiling, butter one side of each slice of white bread with 1 tablespoon of softened butter and toast it in a sauté pan till golden brown on buttered side; flip it and lightly toast the unbuttered side. When the bread is done, place it on a piece of aluminum foil in the bottom of the oven to keep it warm. Remove the cooked burgers, top each with 2 slices of American cheese, and return them to the broiler for 1 more minute. Remove the burger to a plate and let rest for at least 1 minute; 2 minutes is better.

Place 1 piece of toast on each of 2 plates, buttered side down, then top each with 1 piece of lettuce, 2 slices of tomato, pickles, and then the rested burger. Top each with 1 tablespoon of the special sauce and the other piece of toast, buttered side up. Enjoy with lots of napkins and frizzled onions on the side.

When Saugatuck Grain & Grape (40 Railroad Place, Westport; 203-557-9120; saugatuckgrainandgrape.com) opened up shop in its Westport neighborhood in 2010, it signaled a shift from a sleepy commuter train stop to what has become the epicenter of a burgeoning Westport culinary scene, and arguably the entirety of Fairfield County.

Centered on a well-edited collection of artisan wines and spirits, Saugatuck Grain & Grape draws both serious oenophiles as well as fans of cocktail culture. The shop takes a boutique approach to its offerings, presenting its wine as tasteful collections organized by region and stacked on open dark steel shelving. The other half of the shop, a mirror image, treats its spirits, beer, and cordials in much the same carefully curated way. Collections of small-batch bourbons, tequilas, single-malt scotches, and liqueurs are arranged in engaging vignettes drawing attention to the depth of the shop's offerings.

Partners Mimi McLaughlin and Jeff Marron are the couple behind Saugatuck Grain & Grape and the vintage-inspired cocktails they enjoy concocting. Mimi minds the grapes while Jeff looks after the spirits, each engaging in constant research and development. One of their greatest feats is the ability to stoke a similar passion in their customers, who are more likely to trust them with what to purchase, what's new, or what they should try.

Regular tasting events highlight Grain & Grape's collections and wine and spirit knowledge, offering a glimpse into the important network of distillers, distributors, and sommeliers they rely upon, as well as rare tasting opportunities. Where else could you have your pick of forty single-malt scotches to sample and purchase?

The first component of this brain trust is Jeff's research into classic craft cocktails. His approach is inspired by an era when bitters were dispensed by apothecaries, and often mines centuries-old recipes and source ingredients such as falernum, orgeat, and homemade tonic syrups for its ambitious cocktail menu.

New Beginning

(SERVES 1)

2 ounces Knob Creek Rye
1 ounce Nonino Amaro
¼ ounce Galliano
2 bar spoons, or roughly 1 teaspoon
   or ⅛ of an ounce of Gomme Syrup
3 drops salt tincture
3 drops cherry bitters
2 drops lemon bitters
Lemon for garnish

Combine all ingredients in a mixing glass and fill it with ice. Stir until properly diluted and well chilled. Strain into a chilled coupe. With a vegetable peeler, hold a lemon over the coupe and cut a slice of the peel with as little white pith as possible. Then, with the shiny side of the lemon peel facing down toward the glass, pinch the peel to express the lemon oils into the cocktail. Twist the peel and drop it into the cocktail. Sit, sip, relax, and enjoy.

CAROLE PECK'S GOOD NEWS CAFE

694 MAIN STREET SOUTH
WOODBURY, CT 06798
(203) 266-4663
GOOD-NEWS-CAFE.COM
CHEF/OWNER: CAROLE PECK

"Get it to the table, but get it to the table right," is Chef Carole Peck's culinary battle cry.

Rated as one of the United States' top one hundred restaurants by Zagat's, Carole Peck's Good News Cafe in Woodbury has been celebrating upscale comfort food with an affinity for local seasonality for twenty years.

Peck describes her food as "real and natural cooking," using the best-quality ingredients from local sources. She had been using this as her guiding principle for decades before farm-to-table was co-opted into what has become a ubiquitous concept. For Peck it is a way of being; her menu pivots around the seasons and its vegetables, guided by her relationship with nearby farms such as Paint Ridge in Washington, The Farm and Ridgway Farm in Woodbury, and Litchfield's Arethusa Dairy. Peck was in the first graduating class of the Culinary Institute of America in its Hyde Park location in 1973. Following school, she skipped up and down the East Coast before calling both Connecticut and France home. Peck opened the Good News Cafe in 1993 as a way to pare down a high-maintenance cooking style in favor of a more casual and accessible one. It is an approach that embodies how she likes to eat and entertain in her own homes.

The South of France, especially the Provençal countryside, is one of Peck's strongest muses, evident in her food, as well as the colorful decor and decorative touches at the Good News Cafe. She shares her eleventh-century farmhouse with her French husband,

and the home has become a locus for annual culinary trips she hosts for friends and fellow gourmands.

Although there is a great deal given to freshness and change at the cafe, there is one beloved dish that regulars know and love. Best known and often imitated is the Lobster Mac, a rich and cheesy dish with shards of lobster that eschews béchamel in favor of a top-secret trio of cheeses.

THE MARTHA

AVOCADO, BEET, PEA & CUCUMBER SALAD

(SERVES 8)

For the salad:

¾ pound beets

Salt

3 ounces chives or scallions, coarsely cut

¾ cup white wine vinegar

1½ cups vegetable oil

Salt and pepper to taste

½ pound cucumber, peeled and seeded

¼ pound shelled peas, blanched

3 ripe avocados

Metal rings for assembly (optional)

For the horseradish cream (Makes about 3 cups):

2 cups heavy cream

Zest and juice of 2 limes

3 tablespoons grated horseradish

2 tablespoons chopped chives for garnish

To prepare the salad: In a large saucepan, cook the beets covered in boiling salted water until tender. Remove from the heat, drain, and cool. Peel the cooled beets and julienne them with a mandoline or knife.

While the beets are cooking, make the vinaigrette. Blend coarse-cut chives or scallions with the vinegar. Add the oil in a steady stream to emulsify. Season with salt and pepper. Strain through a fine strainer.

Cut the cucumber into a ½-inch dice. Mix with the peas, add ¼ cup of vinaigrette, and toss together.

Cut the avocados in half. Remove the pit, then cut the avocado in a ½-inch dice, by slicing lengthwise then crosswise in its skin. Then remove the flesh with a spoon and combine the resulting avocado cubes with the cucumbers and peas. Toss in additional vinaigrette as necessary. Season to taste with salt and pepper.

To make the horseradish cream: In a bowl, mix the cream with the lime zest and juice. Then whisk to a firm peak. Fold in the horseradish. Serve on top of the salad or on the side, garnished with the chives.

To serve: Mold the beets in the bottom of a ring form. Top with a layer of the cucumber, pea, and avocado mixture. Lastly, if desired, finish with horseradish cream. Remove ring form and serve with additional vinaigrette.

Casa Villa

866 East Main Street, Stamford, CT 06902
182 West Main Street, Stamford, CT 06902
2810 Fairfield Avenue, Bridgeport, CT 06605
CASAVILLARESTAURANT.COM
HACIENDAVILLARESTAURANT.COM
Owner/Chef: Alvino Villa

To appreciate Casa Villa, Stamford's beloved Mexican restaurant, means getting to know owner Alvino Villa and his hometown of Puebla, Mexico. The modest Villa prefers the behind-the-scenes kitchen to the bustling front of the house at his three Fairfield County restaurants.

Moving to the United States at the age of eighteen, Villa began his career as a dishwasher, working his way up the restaurant ranks in New York and Connecticut until he opened his first restaurant in 1999. Drawn to the predominantly Hispanic neighborhood of Stamford's West End, Villa opened his first Casa Villa, which reflected the flavors of his Mexican childhood, in a location where he knew its cuisine would resonate with its neighbors. Its success as a popular take-out spot known for its tacos and other Mexican staples eventually transcended its immediate neighborhood and created the demand that led him to open two additional locations. Casa Villa on East Main, Villa's flagship restaurant with its high ceilings and terra-cotta-colored walls, remains the heart of the trio; the third location, farther east in Bridgeport, is called Hacienda Villa (haciendavillarestaurant.com).

A native of central Mexico, where Puebla is located, Villa credits his heritage as the inspiration for Casa Villa's central Mexican backbone. A combination of experience and research informs Casa Villa's menu, which draws heavily on traditional Puebla recipes such as the city's eponymous mole poblano and its famous *chile relleno en nogada*. But nothing speaks to this culinary focal point as much as Villa's own al pastor taco recipe. Known for its famous taquerias where *al pastor* is served traditionally with meat carved from a standing spit, Puebla is the home of the slow-cooked pork and pineapple taco with its trademark bright yellow color. Villa credits a famous Puebla taqueria for his original *al pastor* recipe, which he has continued to tweak over the years.

This reverence for his home continues in the colorful Talavera pottery adorning the restaurants' shelves and sills and the orange walls and tiled floors that recall the terra-cotta hues and the rich, natural clay of central Mexico.

When asked about his favorite food, Villa is quick to deflect from his own cooking to the family meals of goat *barbacoa* and the freshly made warm tortillas from the *mercado público* of his youth. Conversations with Villa often steer back to the city and perhaps Puebla's most famous dish—*chile relleno en nogada.* This dish, representative of the Mexican flag in its trio of green, red, and white, can be found as a rare special at Casa Villa: a smoky stuffed poblano pepper, covered in a rich and creamy walnut sauce, and finished with pomegranate seeds.

Chile Relleno en Nogada

(SERVES 16)

For the stuffing:

½ cup butter

12 garlic cloves

2 onions

2 pounds ground pork

2 pounds ground beef

2½ cups pitted prunes, chopped

½ cup candied citron

1 cup dried raisins

1 cup dried apricots, chopped

6 large pears, cored, peeled, and finely chopped

6 peaches, seeded, peeled, and finely chopped

4 apples, cored, peeled, and finely chopped

2 cups finely chopped pineapple

6 large tomatoes, finely chopped

1 tablespoon ground cinnamon

½ tablespoon ground cloves

½ tablespoon ground nutmeg

10 bay leaves

6 fresh thyme sprigs 6 fresh marjoram sprigs

1½ tablespoons freshly ground pepper

1 cup dry sherry

1 cup dry white wine

Salt to taste

For the chiles:

32 medium chiles poblanos, roasted, seeded, deveined, and soaked in salted water and vinegar for 6 hours

For the sauce:

200 walnut halves, shelled, or about 4 cups

80 raw almonds, shelled, or about 1 cup

14 ounces cream cheese

7 ounces goat cheese

3 ounces fresh cheese

1 slice bread, crust removed and soaked in a little milk

2 cups heavy cream

1 cup milk

1 tablespoon grated white onion

2 tablespoons sugar

1 tablespoon ground cinnamon

½ cup dry sherry

Salt to taste

For the garnish:

Seeds from 6 pomegranates

1 bunch fresh parsley, leaves removed and chopped

Prepare the stuffing: Melt the butter in a large skillet and brown the garlic and onion. Add ground meats, and sauté until they are no longer red. Stir in all the chopped ingredients. Cook until mixture begins to thicken, about 30 minutes.

Add the cinnamon, cloves, nutmeg, bay leaves, thyme, marjoram, pepper, sherry, and white wine. Simmer, stirring constantly, until the mixture thickens, about 1½ hours. Cool.

Fill the chiles with just enough of the cooled stuffing until full.

Prepare the sauce: Boil the walnuts in water to cover for 5 minutes. Remove them from the water and peel off the skins. (Alternatively, soak the walnuts in cold water overnight and then peel.)

Boil almonds in water to cover for 25 minutes, and soak in cold water. Drain and peel off the skins.

Grind the walnuts and almonds in a food processor. Add the remaining ingredients and process until smooth; the mixture will be thick. Refrigerate until ready to use.

To serve: Top the stuffed chiles with the sauce, served warm, and garnish with pomegranate seeds and fresh parsley.

Tostada de Tinga de Pollo

(SERVES 15)

For the red sauce:

5 dried chiles de árbol
10 dried guajillo chile peppers
½ Vidalia onion
5 garlic cloves
½ tablespoon ground cumin

For the tostada:

2 pounds boiled chicken breast, cooled and shredded
1 Vidalia onion
Canola oil
Refried black beans
Crispy fried corn tortillas
½ head chopped romaine lettuce
1 diced tomato
1 red onion, peeled and sliced
¼ cup crumbled cotija cheese
Sour cream (preferably crema, or Mexican sour cream)
    for garnish

To make the red sauce: Blend the raw peppers, onions, garlic, and cumin together until smooth.

To make the tostada: Caramelize the onions and mix with shredded chicken breast. Sauté the chicken with the red sauce until the sauce is reduced. Let it cool.

To serve: Spread refried black beans on a fried corn tortilla, and top with layers of sautéed chicken, lettuce, tomatoes, red onions, cotija cheese, and Mexican sour cream.

CATCH A HEALTHY HABIT

39 UNQUOWA ROAD
FAIRFIELD, CT 06824
(203) 292-8190
CATCHAHEALTHYHABIT.COM
CHEF/OWNERS: LISA STORCH AND GLEN COLELLO

Part cafe and part hub for healthful food activism, Catch a Healthy Habit in Fairfield is an oasis of raw vegan food for its acolytes and Connecticut omnivores alike. Along the culinary spectrum, there are few, if any, restaurants or cafes that inhabit the strict raw/vegan approach as completely as Catch a Healthy Habit. Eschewing ovens for juicers, the cafe does not raise food temperatures above 115 degrees Fahrenheit, attracting raw foodists as well as customers interested in a healthy respite from their normal diets.

Lisa Storch and Glen Colello are the duo behind Catch a Healthy Habit. As business partners and husband-and-wife team, their shared devotion to both educate and nurture through healthy food led them to launch the cafe. They met taking classes at New York's Institute for Integrated Nutrition, each exploring their respective definitions of healthy cuisine and learning how to embrace that as a culinary professional. As chefs and educators for organic, vegan food, they saw its lack of representation in Connecticut and opened Catch a Healthy Habit in Fairfield in 2009.

Storch, a Culinary Institute of America–trained chef, was a vegetarian when she first attended culinary school. She gravitated toward the pastry curriculum, and she found herself adding further restrictions, such as removing wheat and then dairy from her diet for ethical as well as health reasons. She practices what she preaches and is the creative force behind their menu.

Education is central to the mission of Catch a Healthy Habit. Those who seek to understand more about this approach will find a lively weekly series of speakers, films, prep classes, and events that Colello organizes throughout the year.

"It is more about whole foods and being truthful about foods," says Storch, whose menu is filled with whole foods in three categories: juices, smoothies, and eats. Juices and smoothies are often anchored by the cafe's homemade almond milk. At first glance, "eats" seems like any other menu, with items such as a burger, fajitas, cereal and milk, and pizza and pasta.

One of the biggest misconceptions is that their clientele is strictly raw. Many are curious omnivores, who want to eat healthfully. The second is that it's inaccessible. As these two dishes illustrate, with the right preparation and a few common ingredients, a raw dish here and there is easily within reach.

CHOCOLATE PUDDING
(SERVES 1)

2 avocados, peeled and pits removed
½ cup unsweetened almond milk
¼ cup cacao powder
½ cup maple syrup
½ tablespoon vanilla
¼ teaspoon sea salt
Fresh sliced fruit for serving (optional)

Place all the ingredients in a food processor, and process until smooth. Serve alone or with fresh sliced fruit.

GRATEFUL GREEN SMOOTHIE
(ONE 16-OUNCE SERVING)

1 banana, peeled, frozen, and cut into several pieces
½ pear, peeled, frozen, and cut into several pieces
1 date, pitted
2 stalks kale, stems removed
2 ice cubes
1 cup water

Blend all ingredients until smooth and serve immediately.

Don't let the gilded reputation of Fairfield County fool you: The area is a happy home to some classic diners and humble dives.

The elder statesman of the bunch is the Sycamore Drive-in Restaurant in Bethel (282 Greenwood Avenue; 203-748-2716; sycamoredrivein.com), a half-century-old diner that still serves the same thin French-style steak burgers it did when it first opened in 1948. Flash your lights for carhop service, and be sure to order a Dagwood burger with a root beer float, delivered in a frosty mug based on a secret and beloved root beer recipe passed down from its original owners.

No trip to Stamford's Lakeside Diner (1050 Long Ridge Road; 203-322-2252) is complete without ordering a stack of their sugary doughnuts with a cultlike following, baked fresh and available each morning until they run out.

Westport's beloved dive bar is literally sinking into the Saugatuck River. The Black Duck Cafe (605 Riverside Avenue; 203-227-7978), located on a barge on the Saugatuck River in Westport, is known as much for its burgers, with a list of about a dozen specialty burgers, as for its uneven floor and half-sunken appearance.

The phrase "greasy spoon" was created to describe places such as S&S Dugout (3449 Post Road; 203-255-2579). The lines between comfort food, breakfast, and lunch are blurred in dishes such as breakfast mashed potatoes and hot roast beef sandwiches smothered in gravy.

The line in front of People's Choice in Norwalk (77 Wall Street; 203-838-8272) can get quite long during lunch hours, drawing locals to this Jamaican spot known for Caribbean specialties such as oxtail stew, jerk chicken, and beef patties.

Coffee An' Donut in Westport (343 Main Street; 203-227-3808) may serve more than just coffee and doughnuts, but many of its customers never make it further than their chocolate-glazed cake or coconut-covered twist.

CHOCOPOLOGIE

12 SOUTH MAIN STREET
SOUTH NORWALK, CT 06854
(203) 854-4754
OWNER/CHEF: FRITZ KNIPSCHILDT

Pairing sweet and savory is the masterful domain of chef and maître chocolatier Fritz Knipschildt. A modern chocolatier, Knipschildt bridges this divide at Chocopologie in South Norwalk, a European-style cafe that shares a kitchen with its handcrafted chocolate factory.

A native of Denmark, Knipschildt moved to the United States in 1996, launching Knipschildt Chocolatier and opening his first cafe in 2005. His European background and formal culinary and hotel education in Denmark, along with training in France and Spain, have fused with his American home, resulting in confections and a cafe menu with a strong European provenance and a dash of American edge. The cafe menu is dominated by salads, savory buckwheat crepes, and quiches. A *salade niçoise* and French sandwiches such as the croque madame reflect its strong pull toward France.

A communal table and a series of smaller cafe tables anchor the front dining area, made inviting by warm colors and rich textures. A glass case filled with handmade chocolates and desserts separates a team of busy pastry chefs, who are often bent over their own counters mixing, filling, and finishing the house's signature truffles. A long

counter runs alongside the kitchen, allowing you to enjoy lunch or grab a coffee and watch the mesmerizing procession of chocolate making.

Knipschildt marries raw single-origin chocolate with fresh cream, butter, fruits, nuts, and herbs to produce the company's modern take on traditional European truffles. These handmade chocolates are all made on-site in South Norwalk and can be purchased and paired with their hot chocolate or ice coffee. Shelves and barrels filled to the brim with boxes of chocolates wax and wane with the shop's high holy days of Valentine's Day and Easter.

Although South Norwalk is considered home base, Knipschildt's roughly forty different types of truffles are available at familiar high-end shops such as Balducci's, Whole Foods, and Dean & Deluca, not to mention nearby shops such as Sweet Pierre's in Ridgefield and Espresso Neat (page 84) in Darien.

Chef Knipschildt's recipes are not just for dessert, as his special chef tasting dinners can attest. Devising a recipe that embraces both ends of the sweet and the savory spectrum, Knipschildt pairs grilled tuna with lime-chutney polenta and a white chocolate sauce. And for pure chocolate satiety, his classic truffle delivers. The recipe rewards those who take the time to source great chocolate and embrace the patience required to create these mini masterpieces.

Seared Ahi Tuna and Lime-Chutney Polenta with White Chocolate, Jalapeño & Cilantro Sauce

(SERVES 2)

16 ounces polenta

6 limes

4 ounces simple syrup (see Note)

2 (8-ounce) ahi tuna steaks

Salt and pepper to taste

1 quart heavy cream

24 ounces white chocolate

4 ounces (1 stick) butter

1 bunch fresh cilantro

Chopped jalapeños to taste

Olive oil

Special equipment:

One small ring

Boil the polenta till it is tender and drain. Pour it onto a sheet pan to allow any leftover moisture to evaporate. (Note: The polenta should be cooked until the creaminess is gone and it begins to pull away from the sides of your pan.)

Zest 5 limes, cover, and set aside. Cut the remaining lime in paper-thin slice, add the simple syrup, cover, and set aside.

Rub the tuna steaks with salt and pepper, then cover and set aside.

Bring the heavy cream to a boil. Let cool for 5 minutes, add the chocolate, and whisk to emulsify. Add butter, salt, pepper, half the chopped cilantro, and jalapeños to the spice level you prefer.

Cut the skin off the zested limes and cut out the lime sections. Squeeze the juice from the limes after removing the sections. Place the lime sections and lime juice in a bowl. Stir and set aside. Leave 5 lime sections out for each plate.

Pour the sauce on the center of the plate. Take the polenta from the sheet pan, mix and see that it has the right consistency. Mix in the lime chutney, salt, and pepper. Plate the lime-chutney polenta in a small ring (so it stays in shape) on the left side of the plate.

Sear the tuna quickly on all four sides in hot olive oil. Take the tuna off the pan; let it sit for a minute, then cut it in half. One half stays whole; slice the other half into 5 pieces.

Remove the ring from the lime chutney–polenta and place the solid half of tuna on top. On the right side of the lime chutney–polenta and solid tuna, place the sliced tuna in between the lime fillets. Sprinkle with lime zest and fresh cilantro leaves mixed with a touch of olive oil.

Note: Simple syrup is made from equal amounts of sugar and water. Combine mixture in a pot and bring to a boil.

Dark Chocolate Truffles

MADELEINE

(80 PIECES)

1 quart heavy cream

1¼ cups sugar

2 pounds, 9 ounces 71% Ecuadorian dark chocolate, finely chopped, divided

¼ pound (1 stick) unsalted butter, cubed

Cocoa powder or chopped walnuts for rolling

In a double boiler, combine the heavy cream and sugar and bring to a boil, making sure to dissolve the sugar completely. Once the mixture comes to a boil, slowly add the 2 pounds of chocolate while whisking. When the mixture reaches body temperature and the chocolate is melted, add the butter and whisk until well combined and smooth (this is the ganache). Set the ganache aside in a cool place (not in the refrigerator) until it sets, about 6 hours. Cover the container tightly with plastic wrap and refrigerate for 1 hour.

Roll the chilled ganache into small 1-inch balls and place them in the refrigerator on a parchment-lined sheet pan for approximately 20 minutes.

In the meantime, slowly melt the remaining 9 ounces of dark chocolate in a double boiler and let it cool until it reaches body temperature.

Wearing plastic gloves, dip the ganache ball into the melted chocolate and shake off the excess chocolate. Roll the truffles in cocoa powder or chopped walnuts, shaking off the excess. Allow to set for 5–10 minutes.

Store the truffles in a cool, dry, and dark place. They will keep for approximately a month.

SoNo Marketplace

The SoNo Marketplace is a hive of local food purveyors and artisans, hosting a weekly farmers' market and a summer beer garden. The market's vast 50,000 square-feet, focus on local vendors, and growing roster of food-centric events may be best argument to never set foot inside a super-market again. The vision of founder John Palino who was inspired by the ambience of European-style markets, the SoNo Marketplace sprang to life in an industrial neighbor-hood on Wilson Avenue in South Norwalk. Open each week-end beginning on Friday, the market hums with the energy of more than forty vendors that include area favorites such as Chocopologie, Pasta Fresca, Olivette, Festivities Cater-ing, and Ronnybrook Dairy to name a few.

SONO MARKETPLACE

314 Wilson Avenue, Norwalk, CT; (203) 838-0719;
sonomarketplace.com

COMMUNITY TABLE

223 LITCHFIELD TURNPIKE (US 202)
WASHINGTON, CT 06777
(860) 868-9354
COMMUNITYTABLECT.COM
EXECUTIVE CHEF: JOEL VIEHLAND

In the rural Litchfield County town of Washington, Community Table and its team, led by Executive Chef Joel Viehland, stand at the center of a tight network of farmers, foragers, and discerning diners. Born from agrarian collaboration rather than co-opting it, Community Table was built around the notion that a community restaurant must not only serve its diners, but act with respectful stewardship of the surrounding land.

"You should feel better than when you came in; I want people to feel refreshed," says Viehland, who strives to make the dining experience a restorative pleasure, not a gustatory burden.

Produce and animals all hail from local farms, and the bounty of local foraging trips fill in seasonal gaps with wild greens and vegetables. The restaurant works with local foragers to supply native greens and herbs such as sorrel, lamb's quarters, pennycress, rosehips, and fresh juniper. In-house butchering, salting, pickling, curing, kitchen composting, and the occasional kombucha fermentation experiment complete the circle of hyper-local and seasonal sourcing and research. This focus translates to a daily curated menu that celebrates the natural through its unconventional, yet complementary, pairings and exquisite plating. Creatively deconstructed desserts equally astound, thanks to Tommy Juliano, the restaurant's resident pastry chef.

A community table made from three-hundred-year-old black walnut anchors one of two dining spaces. Witty nods to the restaurant's agrarian ethos surface in art and object, such as a stag-head trophy mount in orange mesh wire and faux-fur animal hides draped across Shaker-inspired chairs.

Chef Viehland studied cooking at Johnson and Wales Culinary School before moving to New York City to work at Gramercy Tavern and, with Chef Katy Spark, at Quilty's, Viehland's inspiration on "how to think and taste." From New York, Viehland moved to New Orleans, a city known for its rich and soulful food heritage of Creole and Cajun cooking, spending ten years making his way through its best kitchens, from Herbsaint to Emeril's and Stella. Trading southern spice for Nordic minimalism, Viehland moved to Copenhagen to work at Noma. The time he spent in its two Michelin-starred kitchen helped him rethink his southern approach to spice and introduced him to foraging, allowing him to define local and seasonal cooking in the strictest sense possible.

The culmination of these experiences—the cultural melting pot of New Orleans and especially the New Nordic focus of Noma culinary lens—explain Chef Viehland's view for creating Connecticut's most radically local menu.

Fallen Leaves Salad with Lemon Verbena–Holy Basil Kombucha, Sorrel & Nasturtium

"We came up with this dish a few years ago. I wanted to create a healthy and different textural experience. It's really a dish like some of our others that is truly inspired by nature. This is completely a fall dish in flavor and feel. It is meant to look like the fallen leaves scattered on the forest floor," says Joel. He also adds, "We use a little of our own kombucha we make at the restaurant, which takes a few months to prepare, but you can make this yourself at home fairly easily. I use a recipe from Sandor Ellix Katz's book called *The Art of Fermentation.* You can obviously make this vinaigrette without kombucha, but I love it, so I use it."

(SERVES 4–6)

For the salad:

2 hot-house tomatoes, sliced

12–15 very thin slices peeled butternut squash

1 large beet, very thinly sliced

2 pears, thinly sliced

2 apples, thinly sliced

1 quince, thinly sliced

8 thin slices watermelon

For the vinaigrette:

4 ounces of lemon verbena and holy basil kombucha (optional)

1 tablespoon Dijon mustard

10 large sorrel leaves

Handful of nasturtium blossoms

Juice of ½ lemon

3–5 ounces grapeseed oil

1–2 ounces of extra-virgin olive oil

For serving:

Handful or two of baby lettuces, preferably red oak, purple curly mustards, and nasturtium leaves

Fresh herbs for garnish (optional)

Sliced raw vegetables for garnish (optional)

Special equipment:

Dehydrator

Blender

Fine strainer

Japanese or French mandoline

To make the salad: Spread out all salad ingredients in an even layer on the dehydrator trays so they do not overlap. Place them in the dehydrator for 6 hours at vegetable setting.

To make the vinaigrette: Place all the ingredients except the oils into a blender minus and blend at a high speed. Slowly add the oils, emulsifying the ingredients. Adjust seasoning with salt, pepper, and lemon juice as needed.

To serve: Arrange the dried vegetables and fruits, and fresh lettuces in a natural way on the plate and lightly drizzle the vinaigrette around the salad. You can garnish further with fresh herbs, if you wish, and maybe with slices of some raw vegetables, too.

CAROMANDEL

25-11 OLD KINGS HIGHWAY, DARIEN, CT 06820
316 SOUTH MAIN STREET, NEWTOWN, CT 06854
86 WASHINGTON STREET, SOUTH NORWALK, CT 06854
68 BROAD STREET, STAMFORD, CT 06901
17 PEASE AVENUE, SOUTHPORT, CT 06890
COROMANDELCUISINE.COM

Inspired Indian home cooking, Coromandel Cuisine of India is a family of six restaurants, with four in Fairfield County, that embraces the subcontinent's traditional dishes with frequent and creative reinvention. What sets the restaurant apart is its emphasis on sourcing traditional recipes from master chefs and dedication to customer service. This nod to history extends to the restaurants' design, where touches of dark wood, vibrant Hindu artwork, and deep earth tones grace most of the dining rooms and white table cloths and attentive service are a consistent presence.

Rooted in tradition, each restaurant respects the disparate culinary roots and deep ties of regional Indian culture and cuisine. Tradition makes up only half the equation of the restaurants' success. They take time to further refine these time-honored recipes, deconstructing them and remaking them as their own.

This begins at its most basic level, with its carefully constructed accompaniments and spiced rices. *Pyaz ki* chutney is Coromandel's take on chutney. Finely chopped onions are marinated with spices, crushed tomatoes, and Indian pickle seasonings, giving it a crunchy bite. Accompanying most dishes is a trio of tomato, tamarind, and lemon basmati rice—a thoughtful treatment of basmatic rice blended with a medley of fruit and spice seasonings.

Tikka masala, a dish that is often considered more British than Indian, is a Coromandel favorite and for good reason. Coromandel's interpretation of the tandoor-cooked dish is chicken broiled in a tandoor oven and finished in a rich *makhani,* a decadent tomato-based sauce cooked with cream and spices like cinnamon, cloves, pepper, fenugreek, and a dash of honey.

Coromandel's popular *sham savera* is an Coromandel specialty that echoes the popular Indian dish, *saag panir.* In this deconstructed dish, *panir* cheese is rolled up in pureed and seasoned spinach, and then steamed into a tight tube that is cut into rolls. *Sham savera* in Hindi means "night and day," a reflection of this dish's stark beauty.

SHAM SAVERA

(SERVES 2)

For the croquette:

1 tablespoon butter (to cook)
1 teaspoon chopped garlic
1 (10-ounce) package frozen spinach, thawed,
    squeezed dry, and chopped
1 potato, peeled and boiled
2 teaspoons all-purpose flour
1 teaspoon bread crumbs

For the panir:

½ pound crumbled panir (a mild Indian cheese)
1 teaspoon ground roasted cumin
1 teaspoon salt

For the sauce:

2 teaspoons sunflower oil
1 teaspoon mustard seeds
¼ teaspoon kasuri methi (fenugreek)
½ teaspoon Madras curry powder
¼ teaspoon tomato ketchup
Pinch of tomato puree
2 tablespoons heavy cream
1 tablespoon honey

2 tablespoons of sunflower oil for frying
Shredded panir for garnish
Cooked basmati rice for serving (optional)

To make the croquette dough: Melt the butter to cook and then lightly brown the garlic. Add the thawed chopped spinach and cook for about 5 minutes.

Once the spinach is cooked take it off the heat, mash and add the boiled potato, and mix well. Add all-purpose flour and bread crumbs to the spinach mix and make a dough.

To make the panir croquette: In a mixing bowl combine the crumbled panir, add cumin and salt, and mix well.

Take a fistful of spinach dough and flatten it with your hands to a 5-inch round. Make small batons (½ inch thick and 2 inches long) of the panir mixture. Place the panir in the center of the spinach patty and roll the spinach over the panir, completely engulfing the panir from all sides. Shape it to a croquette. Repeat with the remaining spinach dough and panir.

Add enough sunflower oil to cover the bottom of the pan. Fry the spinach croquettes on high heat and set aside.

For the sauce: Heat the oil, and add mustard seeds, kasuri methi (fenugreek), Madras curry powder, tomato ketchup, tomato puree, heavy cream, and honey and cook to a thick consistency. Pour the sauce on the serving plate.

Cut the croquette in halves and place them on the sauce. Sprinkle with some shredded panir as garnish. You could serve a spoonful of cooked basmati rice as accompaniment as well.

BADAMI JHINGA

SHRIMP WITH ALMONDS

(SERVES 2)

2 teaspoons sunflower oil
1 teaspoon ginger paste (or powdered ginger)
1 teaspoon chopped garlic
½ red onion, peeled and chopped
1 spring onion (or scallion), chopped
Pinch of turmeric powder
¼ teaspoon biriyani masala (masala powder)
1 tablespoon tomato ketchup
6 raw shrimp
2 tablespoons crushed roasted almonds
Lemon wedges for serving
1 large fresh tomato, chopped

Heat oil and sauté ginger and garlic until lightly brown, add red onion, chopped tomato, spring onion, turmeric powder, and biriyani masala, and cook till masala is cooked. Add tomato ketchup and little water and cook for a few more minutes.

Devein and clean the shrimp and grill on a griddle until shrimp are cooked.

Place the shrimp on the serving plate and pour the sauce over them. Sprinkle the crushed roasted almond slivers over the shrimps and sauce. Serve hot with a lemon wedge on the side.

DaPietro's Restaurant

36 Riverside Avenue
Westport, CT 06880
(203) 454-1213
DaPietros.com
Chef/Owner: Pietro Scotti
Co-Owner: Janine Scotti

A charming dining room filled with the constant presence of the affable chef/owner Pietro Scotti makes the diminutive DaPietro's Restaurant feel more like the comfortable den of a favorite uncle than the intimate dining room of one of Westport's oldest Italian restaurants.

Westport may have changed over the past twenty years, with larger businesses taking the place of small shops, but the jewel box that is DaPietro's has barely budged. Outlasting many of its fellow fine-dining establishments, DaPietro's in Westport has become known as a special occasion spot with a firm grasp of northern Italian dishes and rich pastas.

Housed in just a few hundred square feet, DaPietro's thirty-seat dining room is made even cozier with wood paneling, brass tabletop lamps, and walls adorned with colorful gold-framed Hermes scarves. Pietro Scotti is the Italian-born chef/owner who opened this eponymous restaurant in 1988 after a decades-long tenure at the nearby Cobb's Mill Inn, making it an extension of his home hearth with his personal touches and the welcoming presence of himself and his wife and partner, Janine Scotti.

Born and raised on the island of Ischia in Italy's Gulf of Naples, Chef Pietro Scotti began cooking at age eleven and has hardly left the kitchen since. Leaving home for mandatory military service, Scotti spent his eighteen months in Italy. Smitten with the idea of traveling the globe, he began working as a chef on supertankers, preparing huge meals in his floating dining room, widening his palette as he visited continents that extended far beyond the European continent he once called home.

Those years spent cooking around the world are still evident in his classically refined yet predominantly Italian dishes, which on occasion skew to the south of France and Pacific Rim. Pasta, certainly the seasonally shifting ravioli, is one of Scotti's signature dishes. The ravioli is elevated by the freshest of ingredients, serving as a blank canvas for a fall portrait of flavors such as pumpkin and pignoli nuts.

Ravioli Alla Campagna
with Salsa con Burro a Nocciole

(SERVES 8)

For the filling:

4 ounces goat cheese
4 ounces mascarpone cheese
4 ounces ricotta cheese
1 tablespoon chopped Italian flat-leaf parsley
Pinch of black pepper
Pinch of salt

For the pasta dough:

4 cups flour, divided
¼ cup olive oil
1 teaspoon salt
5 whole eggs, divided
¼ cup water
Semolina flour (for dusting)

Special equipment:

Pasta machine

To make the filling: Mix all ingredients in a bowl and refrigerate.

To make the dough: In a large stainless steel bowl, place 3 cups of the flour, olive oil, salt, 4 of the eggs, and water. Mix until completely incorporated. Cover the dough with a dish towel and let it rest in the refrigerator for 1 hour.

Remove dough from the mixing bowl and cut into four equal pieces. Cover the pieces not being used with the dish towel. Take the first piece of dough and pass it through the pasta machine on the largest setting; repeat this procedure about six to ten times, each time reducing the number on the pasta machine and adding the remaining flour as you go.

Now your pasta sheet is ready to make ravioli. Dust your work surface with some flour and lay the sheet of dough on the flat surface. Beat the remaining egg in a small bowl to use for an egg wash. Brush half of the sheet of pasta with the egg wash and, using a kitchen spoon, place a spoonful of cheese filling on the egg-washed pasta sheet in rows of three. Fold over the empty pasta sheet and seal the edge of each ravioli first with your hands, and follow by cutting it with a form of your choice. Repeat until all the dough is used.

Rest the ravioli in a single layer on a sheet pan dusted with semolina flour. Keep the ravioli covered by a towel before boiling.

Pasta can be frozen for 1 month, or refrigerated for 2 days covered.

For the Salsa con Burro a Nocciole:

4 slices pancetta, diced into ⅓-inch cubes
1½ cups ⅓-inch-dice pumpkin cubes
1 cup (2 sticks) salted butter, sliced
16 fresh sage leaves, halved lengthwise
½ cup pignoli nuts
Salt
2 cups grated Parmesan cheese

Place a large sauté pan over medium heat. When the pan is hot add the diced pancetta and cook until it is brown and crispy. Add the pumpkin and sauté for 2½ minutes until lightly brown. Add the butter and sage leaves. When the butter has melted, add the pignoli nuts. Remove the sauce from the heat.

Bring a large pot of salted water to a rolling boil. Add the ravioli; when the water returns to a boil, cook the ravioli for 1 minute.

Return the sauce to the stove over medium heat.

Use a strainer to remove the ravioli from the pot of water; reserve the cooking water. Place the cooked pasta into either a platter or individual pasta bowls. Evenly sprinkle the ravioli with the Parmesan cheese. When the pignoli nuts in the sauté pan are lightly browned, add 1 cup of reserved pasta water to the sauce. Stir the sauce and then drizzle it evenly over the ravioli.

DRESSING ROOM

27 POWERS COURT
WESTPORT, CT 06880
(203) 226-1114
DRESSINGROOMRESTAURANT.COM
EXECUTIVE CHEF: JON VAAST
OWNER/CHEF: MICHEL NISCHAN

The self-described "homegrown restaurant" The Dressing Room was founded by the late Paul Newman and Michel Nischan in 2006. The restaurant, located adjacent to the iconic Westport Country Playhouse, is the result of a shared vision and determination to create a community gathering place celebrating local, natural, and organic American heirloom food.

Owner Michel Nischan is a James Beard award–winning chef, cookbook author, and sustainable food leader. In addition to launching The Dressing Room, he founded the nonprofit Wholesome Wave, whose mission is to increase production and access to fresh and affordable locally grown food for historically excluded neighborhoods across the country. Overseeing The Dressing Room's kitchen since 2010 is Chef Jon Vaast, who first joined the team as garde-manger and has worked his way up the Dressing Room ranks, becoming executive chef in 2010. When not in its kitchen, you can find him foraging for ingredients at the weekly Westport Farmers' Market or at home brewing his own beer.

The restaurant's gastropub-influenced menu is organized by "small and light" and "medium bites," perfect for sharing and exploration. The restaurant's most coveted dishes remain American classics, such as macaroni and cheese and chopped salads. The "Use a Spoon" chopped salads center around seasonal vegetables cut into small pieces. The name was bestowed by Paul Newman, who preferred a spoon when eating these scoopable salads.

The Dressing Room's take on mac and cheese begins with farmstead Vermont cheddar and cream, and a touch of cured pork belly thrown in for good measure. The pork belly, like all of the restaurant's meats, are pasture-raised by family farmers practicing humane animal husbandry. Pigs and other smaller animals are often broken down by Vaast and the team, whose soft spot for pork is evident in the "Heritage Pork Cut of the Day . . . Jon's daily choice."

Recently, the Dressing Room became one of one hundred American restaurants to participate in "No Goat Left Behind" movement, and Vaast's take on the classic burger speaks to this missive.

Goat Burgers with Bacon & Apple Marmalade

(SERVES 6)

For bacon and apple marmalade (makes 4 cups):

6 peeled Honey Crisp apples, divided

10 cups water

1 cup chopped raw red beets

3 cups cider vinegar

1 cup sugar

1 teaspoon grapeseed oil

2½ cups cubed slab bacon

2½ cups quartered cipollini onions

2 teaspoons mustard seeds, toasted

Salt to taste

For the burgers:

6 jalapeños

2¼ pounds ground goat meat

Salt and pepper to taste

6 brioche buns

1½ cups bacon and apple marmalade (instructions below)

1 cup baby arugula

French fries or salad for serving (optional)

To make the marmalade: Cut 3 apples into quarters, place in medium pot with 10 cups water and 1 cup beets. Bring to a boil and reduce by half.

In a separate pot, combine cider vinegar and sugar, bring to a boil, and reduce by half.

Add grapeseed oil to large sauté pan over medium-high heat, then add the bacon cubes. Once bacon is rendered about halfway add cipollini onions. Caramelize the onions until dark brown, and strain off the fat. Add the toasted mustard seeds.

Combine vinegar reduction and apple reduction then strain it through a fine mesh sieve into a large saucepan.

Add bacon and onion mixture to the reduction and bring to a boil for 10–15 minutes until thick. Core and cube the remaining 3 apples, add them to the saucepan, and continue to cook for 5–10 minutes, until the apples are tender. Remove from heat and add salt to taste. Once cool, you can keep it in the refrigerator for 3 weeks or freeze until ready to use.

To make the burgers: Preheat grill to high.

Grill jalapeños until darkened all around, place in a bowl, and cover with plastic wrap.

Form six 6-ounce goat-meat patties. Season the patties with salt and pepper on both sides, and cook on the grill until medium, about 3–5 minutes on each side.

While the burgers are grilling, toast brioche buns and warm up the marmalade in a small saucepan on the grill.

Remove burgers from the grill. While the meat is resting, clean the roasted jalapeños by removing the skin, stem, and seeds.

Assemble each burger from bottom to top with baby arugula, the burger, marmalade, roasted jalapeños, and then bun top. Serve with a side of fries or a salad.

El Charrito

TRUCK: Richmond Hill Ave, Stamford, CT 06902
TAKEOUT: 7 Apache Drive, Riverside, CT 06878
(203) 940-0922
ELCHARRITOLLC.COM
Co-Owners: Alex and Carlos Terron

One of the most memorable Mexican food experiences in Fairfield County may not be found in a dining room, but on four wheels. Stamford's El Charrito Truck, and its owners Alexandra and Carlos Terron, are a fixture on Richmond Hill Avenue from March through November each year. Carlos originally hails from Mexico, and Alex is Puerto Rican–American. If Carlos is the talent behind the food, Alex is certainly the soul of the operation. She warmly greets every customer and remembers the regulars, offering friendly banter and her infectious smile.

A beacon for fans of traditional Mexican food, El Charrito's traditional and hearty take on Mexican tacos range from *tripa* (chitlins), *carnitas* (slow-cooked pork), *lengua* (cow tongue), *al pastor* (pork with pineapple), *carne adobada* (spicy pork), *cesina* (salty steak), chorizo, *campechano, bistek,* and chicken. Two corn tortillas envelop each taco, which is topped off with chopped raw onion, fresh cilantro, and accompanying lime wedges—a ubiquitous, traditional presentation.

Should one ever tire of the taco, El Charrito also offers diversity in the form of Mexican burgers, quesadillas, burritos, tamales, moles, huaraches, and special tortas, as well as daily rotating specials that can range from the rich *enchiladas en mole rojo,* the seasonal fish tacos, and a *menudo* soup during the cooler weather.

ELEVEN14 KITCHEN

1114 EAST PUTNAM AVENUE
GREENWICH, CT 06878
(203) 698-6980
JHOUSEGREENWICH.COM/GREENWICH-RESTAURANTS-EN.HTML
CHEF: FRANÇOIS KWAKU-DONGO

The JHouse, a boutique hotel in the Riverside section of Greenwich, is home to the sleek eleven14 Kitchen. The hotel's playful layers of lounges filled with contemporary art and modern decor successfully blur the lines between hotel hospitality and dining experience.

Beginning inside the hotel's stark white lobby, a series of eclectic spaces begin to unfold from this welcoming epicenter, beginning with the apothecary-like display of pickled vegetables, vinegars, and oils lining one wall of the hallway, a visual cue of the culinary devotion to come. As the wall continues, it unfolds into an open pantry display kitchen, a glass-walled pastry kitchen, where you're likely to catch a glimpse of the pastry chef and confections in various states of play. Just beyond lies eleven14's kitchen bar and dining room, an expansive space united by a neutral palette of brown and beige, reclaimed wood floors, and a slate-faced wood-burning open hearth. An outdoor bar and dining space spills out just beyond, with an alfresco fireplace begging for year-round revelry.

The seasonal American culinary program of eleven14 is overseen by Chef François Kwaku-Dongo. Chef Kwaku-Dongo's culinary style was formatively influenced by a childhood spent on his grandmother's cocoa farm in Côte d'Ivoire, and honed by years working at Wolfgang Puck's Spago in both West Hollywood and Chicago.

The chef's personal trajectory from family farm to the heart of modern California cuisine is a perfect fit for the style-conscious JHouse. A globally inspired menu executed with local ingredients and wood-fired cooking represents the evolution of Chef Kwaku-Dongo's farm-to-table roots. Taking advantage of the delicate flavors that smoke imparts, many dishes are finished in the wood-fired oven, such as house-made smoked lamb sausage, pizzas, and the roasted vegetables that make their way into salads and accompany entrees.

Chef Kwaku-Dongo mined the archives for one of his favorite duck recipes: "In 2004 when I said goodbye to Wolfgang Puck after twelve years, I had the good fortune to work for a short period with the genius Richard Melman of Lettuce Entertain You. It was a different world working in the corporate world. However, I met Bruce Cost, an interesting man with a vast knowledge on Chinese food. He taught me how to roast duck."

ROAST PEPPERED DUCK BREAST
WITH GRILLED PINEAPPLE

(SERVES 4)

For the duck:

2 each duck breasts
1 teaspoon salt
1 teaspoon black pepper, cracked
½ teaspoon canola oil
1 teaspoon fresh chopped oregano

For the spiced honey:

4 tablespoons honey
1 teaspoon unsalted butter
2 each cinnamon sticks
2 each star anise

For the spiced grilled pineapple:

1 tablespoon unsalted butter
2 each pineapples, peeled, halved, cores removed, and
    sliced ½-inch thick
1 teaspoon cinnamon sugar (about 95 percent sugar
    and 5 percent cinnamon)
2 tablespoons prepared spiced honey

2 tablespoons raisins
2 tablespoons dried apricots, cut into small dice

For the sauce:

½ cup port wine
1 teaspoon shallots, peeled and sliced
1¼ cup duck jus or chicken stock
2 tablespoons prepared spiced honey

Preheat the oven to 300°F.

Season duck breasts with salt, coarsely crushed black pepper, and rub with oil. Panfry the breasts, skin-side down, in an ovenproof pan over low to medium heat and drain off the excess fat. Cook slowly until golden brown. Turn the breasts over, sprinkle oregano on top, and finish off in the preheated oven for 3–7 minutes. Let the meat rest for 10 minutes before slicing.

In a small saucepan, bring honey, butter, cinnamon sticks, and star anise to a simmer over medium heat. Remove from heat, discard cinnamon and star anise, and keep warm.

Brush some butter over the pineapple, sprinkle with cinnamon sugar, and panfry until caramelized all over. Add about 2 tablespoons of prepared spiced honey and let it cook until it bubbles and the honey turns dark brown. Remove from heat.

Turn the pineapple slices over and top with dried fruits. Pour excess spiced honey from the cooking pan over it and finish the fruit off in the 300°F oven for 3 minutes.

Combine the port wine and shallots in a small saucepan and reduce by one-third. Add duck jus or chicken stock and reduce further, just until it coats the back of a spoon. Add remaining 2 tablespoons of spiced honey and incorporate well.

Serve duck breast slices with sauce and pineapple–dried fruit slices.

ELM

73 Elm Street
New Canaan, CT 06840
(203) 920-4994
ELMRESTAURANT.COM
Chef/Owner: Brian Lewis

The seasonally driven elm is an eighty-seat modern American restaurant with a daily-changing menu that celebrates local farms within the heart of downtown New Canaan. A visual and gustatory splurge, elm's sophistication extends from its menu to a stunningly sleek and modern restaurant design.

Chef Brian Lewis, well-known for his collaboration with actor Richard Gere at The Bedford Post Inn's Barn and Farmhouse restaurants, boasts a style largely influenced by experiences working for legendary chefs Jean-Louis Palladin and Marco Pierre White. This experience, combined with an environmentally aware and community-focused approach, draws inspiration from local Connecticut farmers and artisans.

Elm's rigorous menu features locally sourced vegetables and meats, sustainably raised seafood, and house-made pastas. Dishes are creatively conceived and carefully and exquisitely plated. Showcasing Lewis's style is his signature farm egg ravioli with house-made ricotta, burgundy spinach and brown butter, as well as a lobster spaghetti *alla chitarra* with *uni*, Calabrian chiles, and *bottarga di tonno*. Not all is upscale: Skewing a bit bistro is the elmburger. A recent iteration is made with local grass-fed beef from Greyledge Farm grilled over mesquite charcoal and cherrywood, with tomato jam, Gruyère cheese, and Sriracha.

For a complete elm experience, a four-course tasting menu takes guests on a culinary journey through four local farms such as Millstone Farm in Wilton, Connecticut, and Greyledge Farm in Roxbury, Connecticut. This is perhaps the best way to experience the menu as Chef and Owner Brian Lewis envisions.

One of Fairfield County's most elegant and sophisticated dining rooms is as carefully conceived as the menu. A bespoke walnut floor and thoughtful selection of contemporary art set the tone of modern elegance. A midcentury modern–inspired bookshelf delineates the forty-five-seat dining room and serves as backdrop for a sleek bar, and a custom-designed chef's table inhabits an intimate space leading to the immaculate rear kitchen. A ten-seat pewter bar faces a series of cozy booths, anchored by a row of medallion-like wood sculptures hanging on the wall above. The result is warm elegance and classic modernity.

Maple Bacon & Eggs

(SERVES 8)

Robiola fonduta

8 farm eggs, preferably Millstone Farm's, multi-colored

2 ounces heavy cream

2 ounces crème fraîche

Kosher salt to taste

White pepper to taste

Using an egg shell topper, carefully remove the tops of the eggs and empty the eggs into a mixing bowl.

Place the empty eggshells in a bowl with warm water, rinse gently, and then transfer to the reserved eggshell containers, upside down to allow to drain. Let the eggshells dry for about an hour at room temperature.

Using your fingers, gently remove any residue or "skin" left behind in the eggshell. Return to a clean eggshell container and store at room temperature until ready to use.

Place the eggs, cream, and crème fraîche in a stainless steel bowl. Bring a medium size pan of water to a boil and reduce the heat to low. Place the bowl of eggs over the heat and whisk constantly to create very small curds, for about 5 minutes. Be sure to leave the eggs a bit runny, as they will firm up while resting.

Transfer the soft eggs to a disposable plastic pastry bag or thick plastic sandwich storage bag. Place in a warm place near the oven for up to 20 minutes. This egg preparation needs to be made within one hour of service.

Robiola Fonduta

1 pound robiola tre leche cheese

1 cup, heavy cream

Kosher salt, to taste

1 iSi whipped cream charger fitted with 2 c20 charges

Place the cream and robiola cheese in a medium bottom saucepan and place over a very low flame.

Season with salt to taste and melt slowly, stirring until fully melted.

While still warm, transfer to a whipped cream dispenser and seal tightly. Add two co2 chargers and outfit with a small tip.

Hold in a water bath with a thermometer reading 54 c.st.

To Assemble:

8 shelled eggs

8 napkin rings with underliners, to hold and
    serve the eggs

8 soft scrambled eggs

Robiola fonduta

8 paper thin strips of bacon, cooked until crisp in a
    sauté pan and reserved to cool to room temperature.

Maldon sea salt

Bliss maple syrup (or your favorite)

1 tablespoon freshly minced chives

With the egg shells sitting with the open end up in an eggshell container, carefully fill with the soft scrambled eggs ⅔ of the way to the top.

Place the pointed tip of the robiola fonduta charger into the egg and gently disperse until the cheese rises to the top.

Sprinkle with Maldon sea salt, minced chives and a generous drizzle of maple syrup. Place the bacon chip into the side of the egg allowing it to stand.

Serve immediately and enjoy!

ESPRESSO NEAT

20 GROVE STREET
DARIEN, CT 06820
(203) 202-7215
ESPRESSONEAT.COM
OWNER: RACHEL HAUGHEY

Made-to-order coffee is a ritual of details and precision where convenience never trumps quality. At Espresso Neat in Darien, each cup begins from roasted beans no older than forty-eight hours. Once an order is placed, coffee beans are ground, weighed, water temperature is calibrated (between 195°F and 205° F), and each cup of coffee is brewed by hand as a ceramic cup is filled with hot water to keep it warm.

There is a method to the madness: The obsessive attention to detail paired with quality strives for the superlative. Founded by Rachel Haughey and a partner in August 2009, Espresso Neat is their attempt to set the bar for Connecticut's nascent coffee culture that they first experienced in New York City's boroughs.

There are generally two forms of NEAT caffeination, and each begins with high-quality coffee roasters such as Handsome, Sightglass, or Ritual. For espresso-based drinks, shots are pulled from a La Marzocco machine. Shots of espresso and macchiatos (a shot of espresso marked with foam) are paired with a small glass of seltzer. The more milk-loving lattes and cappuccinos are adorned with smooth foam marked with latte art, a signature of a trained barista and a display of properly steamed milk. If a regular drip coffee is what you're after, a timed pour-over extraction from your choice of single-origin beans will produce a perfect cup of coffee that never has sat in a carafe.

Coffee in this pure and obsessive form is central to Espresso Neat's ethos, but teas and snacks are also available from a handful of carefully chosen purveyors, including Norwalk's SoNo Baking Company & Cafe (page 139). In pursuit of spreading the word of caffeine excellence, Neat, as many locals refer to it, is also devoted to education and hosts a number of classes and gatherings. "Home Brewing Basics" and "Brew Methods" focus on producing the perfect cup in your home, as well as traditional "cuppings" or coffee tastings that encourage sniffing, slurping, and occasionally spitting to dive deep into the flavor profiles of the coffee bean.

CLEVERLY DRIPPED COFFEE

(SERVES 1–2)

21 grams fresh whole bean coffee (preferably roasted within the past 14 days)
Good-quality water (see note 1 below)

Special equipment:

Kettle for boiling/pouring water
Metric kitchen scale
Melitta #4 filter, white or unbleached
Clever Coffee Dripper
Burr coffee grinder (see note 2)
Timer
Wooden stir stick
Mug or small carafe/pitcher (make sure the Clever fits on the rim!)

Start heating the water in the kettle. You'll need 340 grams (about 12 ounces) for brewing plus a bit more for preheating and rinsing.

Meanwhile, measure out 21 grams of coffee. Generally speaking, the ideal ratio to target for brewing coffee is around 60 grams of coffee per 1,000 grams (1 liter) of water.

Place your coffee filter in the Clever and rinse with a bit of the boiling water. This not only removes the paper taste from the filter, but also preheats the Clever.

Grind your coffee at a medium setting, and add it to the rinsed and drained filter. The particle size should be finer than sea salt but coarser than table salt. Place the coffee-filled Clever on your scale and tare it to zero.

Allow your water to rest for about 15 seconds off the boil in order to come down in temperature a bit. The ideal temperature for brewing coffee is between 195°F and 205°F. When ready, take the kettle in one hand and your timer in the other. Start the timer and wet the coffee grounds with about 40–50 grams of hot water.

Assuming your coffee is freshly roasted, you'll notice the grounds "bloom" or expand a bit as they release carbon dioxide (CO_2). Once your timer hits 15 seconds, start pouring in the rest of the water (total will be 340 grams), aiming to finish pouring by 30 seconds (so a 15-second pour). You'll notice a "crust" of coffee grounds form on top.

At the 1-minute mark, use your wooden stir stick to break this crust by making the shape of an N and then a Z. By using this standardized stir, you are better able to have consistent agitation (and therefore a consistent cup of coffee) from brew to brew.

When the timer reaches 2:30, set the Clever on top of your mug or carafe.

If your grind is correct, the coffee should finish draining at about the 3:45–4:00 minute mark on your timer. If it is significantly slower (or faster), try adjusting your grind coarser (or finer) to correct the total contact time.

Oh, and cleanup is a snap. Just toss out the filter and grounds (both can be composted!), give your Clever a good rinse under hot water, and set it out to dry.

Note 1: Your final cup of coffee is more than 98 percent water, so the quality of the water you use is important, both for its inherent flavor and

the way it affects the extraction of the coffee. It should be odorless, free of any visible impurities, and not overly hard or soft. If in doubt, try using Volvic bottled water and do a side-by-side taste comparison.

Note 2: A good burr grinder is potentially the most important component for brewing a tasty cup!

COFFEE ROASTERS

For three Connecticut businesses, great coffee begins with great beans. Redding Roasters in Bethel (81 Greenwood Avenue; reddingroasters .com) is one such institution. A simple operation that sells its single origin beans out of its small shop, it also wholesales to customers including Bethel's O'Neill's and Ridgefield's Tusk & Cup.

Stamford's Raus Coffee (rauscoffee.com) sells its beans and cold coffee drinks at farmers' markets and Westport's Steam Coffee Bar. Donny Raus is the founder and owner of Raus Coffee, as well as the driving force behind its mission of sourcing its sustainably grown beans around the world. His espresso blend is the foundation for Raus's popular ice coffee drinks such as the Cold Roman and Roman Kiss, which are available bottled.

In New Canaan, the siren-call aroma of Doug Zumbach's roaster pervades the downtown (Zumbach's, 77 Pine Street; zumbachscoffee.com). The coffee shop sells coffee—single-origin, blends, and flavored—and brews excellent cups of coffee and espresso. The spartan shop is devoted to coffee; little else adorns its shelves and walls other than coffee beans themselves. A fan of vintage cars, Zumbach's is also ground zero for Caffeine and Carburetors (caffeineandcarburetors.com), a bimonthly gathering of car enthusiasts that draws thousands.

Fat Cat Pie Company

9–11 Wall Street
Norwalk, CT 06850
(203) 523-0389
FATCATPIE.COM
Chef: Robert Herlihy

Fat Cat's famously thin crust and vast wine list may have put them on the Norwalk dining map, but their towering salads and an enticing breakfast may be their best-kept secrets.

Founded by Mark Ancona and Anthony "Tony" Ancona, with their father, Stephen, Fat Cat first opened in 1993 as a modest yet energetic bistro focused on pizza. Housed in a historic theater building replete with exposed brick walls and open ceilings, Fat Cat's kitchen is overseen by Chef Robert Herlihy, whose fresh-from-the-garden take on pizza pairs well with Fat Cat's signature wafery-thin crusts. The pizzas are laden with local produce from Westport's Double L Market, fresh and aged cheeses, and inventive combinations of ingredients. One of the most famous dishes at Fat Cat doesn't even have a crust. The kale and quinoa salad is one of several fresh green salads, in addition to artisanal cheeses and homemade soups, that round out the small but satisfying lunch and dinner menu.

Creeping into morning hours, Fat Cat sheds its lively wine and pizza persona for their

signature take on mornings, with thirteen-inch breakfast "pizzas" that replace sauce and cheese with eggs and sausage, a selection of house-made baked goods, and homemade granola, paired with espresso drinks.

As Tony Ancona explains, "We never intended this to be just a pizza place." Over the years, the restaurant grew its related wine business, Fountainhead Wines & Distillations, ensuring that Fat Cat's reputation would grow beyond pizza. The wine program is led by Michael Pelletier, an Ancona high school friend, who shares the family's history of food and wine.

Located across the street from Fat Cat, Fountainhead Wines & Distillations focuses on a hand-picked collection of small production wines, placing the importance on price and style over region. With a deep appreciation for winemakers, Fountainhead imports from about forty producers and still works with the original six producers who were with them at the beginning. The benefits of this business symbiosis appears on Fat Cat's impressively diverse wine selection—a list of twenty wines by the glass, over three hundred bottles spanning fifteen varietals, and even Fat Cat's own private-labeled wines.

Chef Herlihy may best be known for his thin-crust pizzas and towering salads, but his butterscotch pudding recipe has garnered a cultlike following with its pitch-perfect balance of sweet and salty.

FCP Butterscotch Pudding

(SERVES 4–6)

1 quart heavy cream
2 cups whole milk
⅓ cup packed dark brown sugar
2 teaspoons salt
2 teaspoons vanilla extract
12 egg yolks
1 cup granulated sugar
¼ cup water
Crème fraîche or whipped cream for serving

Special equipment:

12 (6-ounce) ramekins or custard cups
Shallow baking pan for water bath
Aluminum foil

Preheat oven to 400°F.

In a saucepan combine cream, milk, brown sugar, salt, and vanilla. Place on the stove over medium heat.

Place all the egg yolks (completely white-free) in a bowl.

While the cream is heating, caramelize the granulated sugar in a saucepan with the water. To do this, simply place the saucepan over high heat till the sugar begins to caramelize and becomes a deep copper color. (Note: If you cook the sugar too long and burn it dark brown, your pudding will have an unpleasant burnt taste.)

When the sugar is caramelized, working quickly but carefully, pour it into the hot cream. A small thermal explosion will occur when you do this, so take care not to burn yourself. If the sugar becomes a huge hard ball when added to the

cream, it means that your cream was not hot enough, but no problem—just put the mixture back on the stove until the sugar dissolves. When you have a nice amber liquid of sugary cream, it's time to add the eggs.

With a ladle, temper the yolks before adding them to the hot cream by slowly adding some of the hot cream mixture first to the egg yolks, whisking the yolks. Add two or three ladles of cream like this, then steadily add this egg mixture to the hot cream-sugar solution. Whisk to combine slowly–– so no bubbles.

Strain this mixture through a mesh colander into something that will allow you to pour it, like a big pitcher.

Pour the uncooked pudding into twelve custard cups evenly and carefully; these vessels are also the serving bowls. Have enough boiling or very, very hot water to pour into the bottom of your shallow baking dish, coming about one quarter

of the way up. Place the puddings into the water, watching the displacement; the water should come about halfway up the outside of the cups now.

Cover the entire baking dish tightly with foil to keep the steam in. They will steam in the oven, which is why the water has to be very, very hot to start and the foil has to be airtight (or near enough).

Bake at 400°F for 15–20 minutes.

After 15 minutes give a look, but be careful: Steam burns are the worst! The puddings should appear a lot less liquid but still "jiggly" in the middle. If they are overcooked they will look bubbly and separated—not good. When done, take the puddings out of the oven and uncover them. When cool enough to handle, place each individually into the fridge. They'll firm up more as they cool.

Serve alone or with a dollop of either crème fraîche or whipped cream. Enjoy!

Hanna's

72 Lake Avenue
Danbury, CT 06810
(203) 748-5713
hannasofdanbury.com
Owner: John Hanna

Tabouli, kibbe, and hummus are just a few of the Lebanese staples found on the shelves and on the menu at Hanna's Middle Eastern Restaurant and Deli. One part restaurant, one part market and deli, Hanna's has been a Danbury beacon of Middle Eastern ingredients for over twenty years since first opening on Lake Avenue. Owner John Hanna began working in restaurants in his home country of Lebanon before moving to New York in 1977. Moving north to Danbury, he opened Hanna's in 1989. In addition to selling prepared foods, including falafel, tabouli, kibbe, and spinach pies (as well as everything on the restaurant menu), the shop also sells Middle Eastern ingredients such as grains, spices, pickles, olives, and cheeses.

The market proved so popular with its regulars, from Danbury natives to homesick customers who grew up in the Middle East and craved the taste of home, that Hanna

opened an adjoining restaurant three years later. The symbiosis of the restaurant and the market, which sells many of the ingredients found next door—halloumi, harissa, olives—is a perfect trove of inspiration and Middle Eastern staples if you're feeling adventurous enough to re-create your meal.

The restaurant is a small and casual place with framed posters of Lebanese landscapes and cultural mementos scattered across its walls. Meza, or appetizers, such as hummus, baba ghannoush, and moussaka; salads; kebabs, and classic Lebanese dishes, such as stuffed grape leaves and squash, shish tawook (marinated chicken served over rice), and baked kibbe make up the traditional backbone of Hanna's menu. Desserts are another of Hanna's specialties, including backlava (Hanna's version of baklava is made with cashews), rice pudding, and *knafeh,* a sweet and sticky shredded pastry layered with cheese. Strong Turkish coffee and its less-robust replacement white coffee (a combination of hot water, orange blossom water, and, often, sugar) is an appropriate end to a Hanna's meal.

Tradition and consistency reigns at Hanna's, and little has changed in two decades, a fact that makes owner John Hanna quite proud. Kibbe, which can be served raw or baked, is one example of the traditional recipes Hanna's celebrates.

Baked Kibbe

(SERVES 6–8)

Stuffing layer

1½ pounds ground beef or lamb (or mixed)
1 onion
1 teaspoon allspice
1 teaspoon black pepper
1 teaspoon salt
About 1 cup of toasted pine nuts
Olive oil for the pan

Kibbe layer

2 pounds lean ground beef
2 pounds fine bulgur, soaked
1 grated onion
1 teaspoon ground allspice
1 teaspoon ground black pepper
1 teaspoon salt

For the stuffing layer: Dice the onion very small and sauté it in a large skillet in about 1–2 tablespoons of olive oil. Add the ground meat and seasoning, cooking the meat until browned. Then mix in the pine nuts.

For the kibbe layer: Mix the bulgur with salt and pepper and allspice, then add onion and the meat. Mix it very well. Add small amounts of cold water as you mix until you get the desired texture, not too soft and not too hard.

To bake: Place one kibbe layer ½ cm thick in a 12 x 17-inch tray brushed with oil. You cover it with a layer of stuffing. Then you put another kibbe layer over it at the same ½ cm thickness. Score the top with a knife to make it look like small diamond-shaped pieces. Brush with a little oil on top and bake for 45 minutes at 360°F.

L'escale

500 Steamboat Road
Greenwich, CT 06830
(203) 661-4600
LESCALERESTAURANT.COM
Executive Chef: Frederic Kieffer
Owner: Rick Wahlstedt

L'escale is a beacon for Fairfield County Francophile gourmandise. Embracing its namesake—*l'escale* means "port of call" in French—its inimitable Greenwich harbor location informs a seafood-centric Provençal menu and draws a posh crowd befitting its zip code.

Local fish and shellfish with classic Provençal ingredients and preparations are the familiar trademarks of L'escale's Gallic refinement. Summer meals at L'escale's are often enjoyed on the 2,500-square-foot outdoor deck and bar, with the centrally located Le Bar á Huître, a custom-designed raw bar, often piled high with Thimble Island oysters, bivalves, and crustaceans. Fittingly, the entire menu is a seafood-dominated symphony of dishes, beginning with an ambitious list of raw-bar offerings that culminates in the the Plateau Royal, a towering pièce de résistance of lobster, oysters, scallops, shrimp, and mussels.

Classic French dishes cascade from the menu: tartare de boeuf, a traditional steak tartare served with potato chips; Dover sole; Chef Kieffer's celebrated bouillabaisse; and escargot en croute, not to mention the dozens of other Provençal dishes marked by a smattering of fresh herbs and seasonal vegetables.

Leading this singularly French menu is Executive Chef Frederic Kieffer. Born and raised in Paris, his culinary education was burnished at L'École Superieure de

Cuisine Française Ferrandi in Paris, where he trained in classical French cuisine. Working in the renowned Parisian restaurants Taillevent and Le Chiberta, he moved to the United States to work on projects in Los Angeles and New York before settling in Fairfield. Today Kieffer splits his time between both Artisan (page 4) and L'escale, dominating southern Fairfield County's appetite for Provençal cuisine.

Many L'escale recipes are *voyage instantané* in a dish, and nothing represents this better than the bouillabaisse *traditionelle,* a mouthful of ocean with a saffron-lobster broth studded with calamari, prawns, clams, and mussels.

BOUILLABAISSE

(SERVES 8)

For the bouquet garni:

½ bunch parsley
10 fresh thyme sprigs
5 bay leaves

For the fish soup base (makes 6 quarts):

5 pounds lobster shells
¾ cup olive oil, divided
2 heads fennel, chopped
1 chopped onion
1 head garlic, split in half crosswise
2 pounds fish bones (bass, fluke, sole)
1 pound fish scraps (small pieces, including fish tail or belly)
1 cup Ricard
2 cups white wine
2 cups clam juice
2 large cans whole Italian plum tomatoes
12 ounces tomato paste
Pinch of cayenne pepper
1 teaspoon paprika
Salt to taste
2 pinches saffron
1 teaspoon herbes de Provence

For the rouille (makes about 5 cups):

8 medium garlic cloves, raw
6 egg yolks
2 pinches saffron
Pinch of cayenne pepper
Salt to taste
2 tablespoons fresh lemon juice
4 cups extra-virgin olive oil

For the bouillabaisse:

16 small Yukon Gold potatoes, peeled
Salt
4 pinches saffron, divided
8 medium garlic cloves, peeled and whole
1 sprig rosemary
2 heads fennel
2 tablespoons olive oil to cook the fennel
80 ounces of fish soup base (recipe above)
16 littleneck clams
40–48 mussels
1½ ounces bass or halibut
1½ ounces grouper or snapper
1½ ounces monkfish
8 Stonington scallops
8 head-on Maya prawns
4 tablespoons olive oil to cook fish

1 pound fresh calamari

½ bunch chopped parsley, plus additional for garnish

1 tablespoon Ricard for deglazing

Rouille (see recipe)

24 garlic croutons (toasted baguette slices rubbed with raw garlic on one side)

Gruyère, shredded for topping

To prepare the bouquet: Wash the parsley. Lay half of it down and place the thyme sprigs and bay leaves on it. Top with the remaining parsley and tie it to resemble a little bundle.

To prepare the fish soup base: Cut the lobster shells into small pieces. Sauté the lobster shells with ½ cup olive oil until golden brown.

Remove the lobster shells, add ¼ cup of olive oil and sauté the fennel, onion, and garlic until light brown. Add the fish bones and cook for about 5–7 minutes.

Place the lobster shells back in the pot, add the fish scraps, and deglaze the pan with the Ricard; reduce by half. Add the white wine, water, clam juice, bouquet garni, tomato products, and all the spices.

Simmer for 1½ hours. Check the seasoning, blend and strain twice through a mesh sieve. Cool over ice.

To make rouille sauce: Prepare the rouille sauce not long before you are ready to serve the Bouillabaisse. In a food processor add the garlic, egg yolk, saffron, cayenne pepper, salt, and lemon juice. Pulse until smooth. As you continue to pulse, slowly add the oil and mix until thickened.

To make the bouillabaisse: Cook the Yukon Gold potatoes in salted water with 1 pinch of saffron, garlic, and rosemary for about 15 minutes.

Cut the fennel into ¼-inch-thick slices and sauté them over medium heat in 2 tablespoons olive oil with 1 pinch of saffron until tender. Reheat the fish soup base with the clams and potatoes for 5–7 minutes. Add the mussels to the fish soup base.

Season the fish, scallops, and shrimp, and sauté them in 4 tablespoons olive oil. When almost cooked, add the sautéed fennel slices and cook for 1 minute. Add the calamari and chopped parsley, and deglaze with 1 tablespoon of Ricard.

To serve: Arrange the fish first in bowl, and ladle the soup with potatoes, clams, and mussels over it. Top with 3 croutons, a ladle of rouille, and shredded Gruyère cheese, and garnish with a little chopped parsley.

LA ZINGARA

8 P. T. BARNUM SQUARE
BETHEL, CT 06801
(203) 852-1088
CHEF/OWNER: TOM GIUDICE
OWNER: LISA TASSONE

Located in the heart of one of Fairfield County's smallest towns is one of its best-kept Italian secrets. La Zingara in Bethel was opened by the husband-and-wife team of Chef Tom Giudice and Lisa Tassone in 2002. It continues to hum as the town's most popular restaurant nearly a decade later with the addition of a newly opened rooftop patio.

La Zingara, Tassone's family nickname, means "gypsy" in Italian. Fittingly, the menu wanders through Italy, tracing the regions as the seasons change and ingredients wax and wane. Dishes are rustic yet refined with the new Ecco rooftop bar ushering in a slightly more relaxed menu centered around wood-fired pizzas.

Along with their veteran staff, the owners are a warm and disarming presence. The couple met on the job, and nine years and two young children later they treat La Zingara and its staff and regulars much like an extended family. Inside the yellow stucco building,

trattoria informality with richly hued red and mustard-yellow walls meets more formal ristorante, replete with white tablecloths and a serious Italian wine list.

Regional Italian, in Chef Giudice's southern Italian hands, means creative and rich compositions served in comforting portions. The *calamari affumicati* is a sautéed calamari served in a smoked tomato broth with arugula and finished with white truffle oil. *Fegato alla Veneziana,* calf's liver sautéed with caramelized onions, is drizzled with a balsamic reduction. All pasta is house-made, ranging from savory-filled crepes to a wild boar ragù served with *pasta al ceppo.* Regulars know to trust the specials, which change daily based on the ingredients at hand.

La Zingara cultivates a 126-acre organic farm in New York where they grow mostly garlic. At nearby Cherry Grove Farm in Newtown, they sharecrop, growing fifty to sixty heirloom tomatoes; nearly twenty thousand tomatoes were cultivated last year. An annual harvest dinner at the Newtown farm celebrates their bounty.

Quaglie Ripieni con Polenta e Spinaci

STUFFED QUAIL WITH POLENTA & SPINACH

(SERVES 4)

For the quail:

1 pound sweet Italian sausage
½ cup toasted pine nuts
½ cup dry currants
½ cup grated Parmigiano Reggiano
Salt and pepper to taste
4 semi-boneless quail
8 slices thick-cut speck (or bacon)
3 tablespoons olive oil

For the polenta:

6 cups chicken stock
2 teaspoons salt
1¾ cups white cornmeal
3 tablespoons unsalted butter
8 ounces diced Taleggio cheese
1 tablespoon olive oil
1 (16-ounce) package fresh baby spinach
2 tablespoons saba or mosto cotto
    (grape must reduction)

Preheat oven to 350°F.

To prepare the quail: Remove sausage from casing. In a large bowl combine sausage, pine nuts, currants, Parmigiano Reggiano, and salt and pepper. Mix until all ingredients are well combined. Separate sausage mixture into four equal portions. Stuff the cavity of each quail with one portion of the sausage mixture. Wrap each quail in a cross pattern with 2 slices of speck, meeting the ends of speck on the bottom side of quail. Set aside.

In a large ovenproof sauté pan, heat olive oil over medium-high heat. Once oil is almost to the smoking point, place the quails in the pan, bottom side down, for approximately 4 minutes or until browned. This should sear speck together. Turn the quails over and brown for another 4 minutes. Place the pan in preheated oven for approximately 10–15 minutes.

To make the polenta: Bring 6 cups of stock to a boil in a heavy, large saucepan. Add 2 teaspoons of salt. Gradually whisk in the cornmeal. Reduce the heat to low and cook until the mixture thickens and the cornmeal is tender, stirring often, about 15 minutes. Turn off the heat. Add the butter and Taleggio, and stir until melted.

In a large sauté pan, heat the olive oil. Add spinach and toss until wilted, about 5 minutes.

To serve: Place the polenta on the bottom of a serving bowl. Top with the wilted spinach and quail. Drizzle with saba and serve.

Nuccia and Andrea Mazzonetto opened Gelatissimo on New Canaan's Forest Street in 2005. Their hand-mixed artisan gelato is made fresh each day in small batches by Ms. Mazzonetto, who learned the technique in Italy. In summer, fresh fruits form the basis of popular flavors such as watermelon and rhubarb, with pumpkin and fig in the fall and seasonless favorites such as hazelnut, pistachio, and chocolate are available year-round.

Sweet Ashley's of Norwalk has served over forty different handmade flavors, all churned on premises for the past twenty years. Named after the owner's eldest daughter, Ashley's is also known for its custom ice cream cakes and inventive seasonal flavors such as Orchard Cherry and Caramel Apple Cider Doughnut. They invite their customers to suggest flavors, which often make it into their flavor rotation.

Ferris Acres Creamery, an 80-acre dairy farm in Newtown, has been attracting ice cream lovers since it began selling ice cream in 2004. Its farm-inspired flavors include Cow Trax (peanut butter ice cream with caramel swirls and mini chocolate chips), Route 302 Moo (chocolate ice cream with swirls of fudge and chocolate chips), and Camp Fire (vanilla ice cream with marshmallow, chocolate chunks, and crushed graham crackers).

A short and very sweet selection of eight ice cream flavors is available on any given day inside Dr. Mike's Bethel shop. Their signature Chocolate Lace and Cream is always on the menu, a combination of creamy vanilla and shards of brittle hard chocolate and caramel "lace" made by Hauser Chocolatiers across the street.

Located in Bridgeport's Black Rock neighborhood, Timothy's corners the market on old fashioned ice cream and fresh waffle cones. Their classic flavors such as Dutch Chocolate, Strawberry, and French Vanilla form the basis of a classic menu of 20 flavors.

Dr. Mike's
158 Greenwood Avenue, Bethel, CT; (203) 792-4388

Ferris Acres Creamery
144 Sugar Street (Route 202), Newtown, CT; (203) 426-8803; ferrisacrescreamery.com

Gelatissimo Artisan Gelato
26 Forest Street, New Canaan, CT; (203) 966-5000; gelatissimoartisangelato.com

Sweet Ashley's Ice Cream Shoppe
248 East Avenue, Norwalk, CT; (203) 866-7740; sweetashleysicecream.com

Timothy's
2974 Fairfield Ave, Bridgeport, CT; 203-366-7496
http://timothysicecream.weebly.com

leFarm

256 Post Road
Westport, CT 06880
(203) 557-3701
LEFARMWESTPORT.COM
Chef/Owner: Bill Taibe

Eat well'

lefarm The whelk

The James Beard–nominated chef Bill Taibe needs no introduction in this neck of the Connecticut woods. Taibe cooked his way around Fairfield County before calling Westport home and launching leFarm, which has garnered numerous critical acclaims since opening in 2009.

The upscale barn-chic dining room at leFarm suits Taibe's farm-centric comfort food with its penchant for fat and offal. His expressive cooking style is at home with the restaurant's focus on all-natural ingredients and its devotion to sourcing from and supporting local farms and purveyors. The restaurant's menu changes frequently and has inspired a series of underground dining events in Fairfield County called "Souterrain," further challenging our notions of dining, and inspiring culinary exploration. Seating about thirty-four, the intimate dining room is outfitted in a neutral color palette of off-whites and

farmhouse touches, such as white plank walls, cheesecloth table coverings, and bean-filled mason jars for your utensils.

Taibe's appreciation for food began early, working at a local butcher shop after school, and intensified as he worked his way through restaurants in Westchester and Fairfield Counties, earning cooking accolades and appearances on *The Martha Stewart Show* along the way.

Rustic preparations of refined ingredients abound, such as the kitchen's often requested Whipped Chicken Livers served with bacon jam on potato-rosemary toast. The leFarm menu changes frequently, although a few steady favorites remain for the ride, such as the Gulf shrimp and cheddar grits, a northern take on a southern classic finished with jalapeños and "fronions," or crispy onion rings. Pork is a consistent ingredient across the leFarm menu, anchoring many dishes as both star and accompaniment. This treatment is likely best prepared in the summer when vegetables, especially corn, are at their peak but can easily be remade into a seasonal dish with various vegetables. The burrata is an ideal appetizer year-round, taking its cue in this recipe from summer squash and fragrant onion bread.

Burrata with Sweet & Sour Summer Squash

(SERVES 4)

For burrata:

4 pieces burrata (about 6 ounces of burrata)
Salt and pepper to taste

For sweet & sour squash:

½ cup sugar
½ cup Cabernet vinegar
2 tablespoons olive oil
2 large zucchini or 4 large summer squash, diced large

To prepare the burrata: Tear or cut open burrata and place on plate, season with salt and pepper.

To make the squash: In a saucepan combine sugar and vinegar and bring to a boil.

Heat a sauté pan and add olive oil. Slowly sauté squash on medium heat until browned and cooked.

Add vinegar and sugar mixture to sauté pan and cook for 1 minute.

To finish: Put sweet & sour squash on top of the burrata. Serve with a piece of toasted onion bread.

BRINED PORK CHOPS
WITH CORN & PEPPER CHOW-CHOW

(SERVES 4)

For the brined pork:

3 cups water

1½ cups salt

½ cup sugar

1 tablespoon black peppercorns

1 tablespoon juniper berries

1 thyme sprig

1 bay leaf

4 pork chops, preferably bone-in

For the corn & pepper chow-chow:

¼ cup sugar

¼ cup seasoned rice vinegar

2 cups diced sweet peppers

1 jalapeño, diced

1 cup roasted corn kernels (cut from the cob;
   see roasting instructions below)

1 tablespoon chopped fresh chives

For the pork chops:

1 tablespoon olive oil

4 brined pork chops (see recipe),
   dried on a paper towel

3 tablespoons unsalted butter

1 clove garlic, minced

1 thyme sprig

To make the brined pork: Put all ingredients (except the pork chops) in a saucepan and bring to a boil. Cool the brine. Pour over pork chops, cover and refrigerate overnight.

To make the roasted corn: Wrap each ear of corn tightly in aluminum foil with the silk removed but husks retained. Place on a hot grill. Cook approximately 30 minutes, turning occasionally, until corn is tender. Remove husks, and cut corn from the cob.

To make the chow-chow: In a saucepan combine the sugar and rice vinegar and heat. Add diced peppers and jalapeño. Cook until liquid is mostly reduced. Add roasted corn and finish with chives

To make the pork chops: Heat a large sauté pan. Add olive oil and brined pork chops. Cook over medium high heat until all sides are a nice brown color.

Add butter, garlic, and thyme. Continue cooking until pork is desired temperature (use a meat thermometer—times change depending on desired temperature and thickness of pork; it should be at least 145°F).

To serve: Plate each pork chop. Add corn pepper chow-chow and drizzle with cooking sauce.

Burgers

New Haven, just to the east of Fairfield County, is often considered the home of the hamburger thanks to Louis' Lunch, its self-proclaimed "birthplace of the hamburger sandwich." So it seems only natural that nearby Fairfield County would take their burgers seriously. At one end of the dining spectrum are a series of elite burgers that source dry-aged beef, freshly made bakery buns, and a variety of intricate toppings. Napa & Co. (page 121), leFarm (page 102), The Spread (thespreadsono.com), and Nicholas Roberts (page 126) have cornered this end of the spectrum with the signature burgers in constant rotation on their menu.

But none have given the burger its own night like South Norwalk's Match Restaurant (page 110). Chef Matt Storch owns Thursday as Norwalk's burger night; his burger tops the menu until it runs out. The burger is constructed with local meat from Greyledge Farm in nearby Roxbury, Connecticut, house-made cheddar-bacon béchamel sauce, caramelized onions, and a touch of balsamic vinegar on an onion brioche bun.

Station Eats in New Canaan and Stamford (stationeats.com), Shake Shack in Westport (shakeshack.com), and Burgers, Shakes & Fries (page 40) are three spots, in some cases with multiple locations, that trade decadence for smaller portions, simpler ingredients, and fast and family-friendly service. Newcomer Station Eats sources organic, grass-fed, and antibiotic- and hormone-free meats as well as vegetarian alternatives, forcing us to rethink the unhealthy trope of the fast food burger.

Liana's Trattoria

591 Tunxis Hill Road
Fairfield, CT 06825
(203) 368-1235
www.facebook.com/lianastrattoria
Chef/Owner: Liana DeMeglio

The embodiment of classic Italian cooking, Liana's Trattoria is the type of cozy Italian spot you're more likely to discover while exploring the Bay of Naples than the Connecticut coastal town of Fairfield. Liana DeMeglio is the warm and welcoming matriarchal presence at the heart of this Italian restaurant, with its reverence for quality ingredients and classic Italian recipes. DeMeglio was born in Padua but raised in Naples, where her appreciation for food and a love of baking began. "I like real food, and as an Italian that's all I know how to make," says DeMeglio. This straightforward approach, honed for the past twelve years, translates to a consistent menu of rustic yet refined antipasti, pasta, hearty entrees, and desserts that are anything but simple in their craftsmanship.

A long-time chef at Pasta Nostra in South Norwalk, DeMeglio worked in Chef Joe Bruno's kitchen for its first ten years, learning from his exacting style and deference for perfectly sourced ingredients. As DeMeglio recounts, it was also Bruno who helped ensure her success by encouraging his own patrons to visit her new restaurant while Pasta Nostra was closed for vacation. That gracious endorsement drew some of her first diners, but it was the quality and consistency of her food, not to mention her tireless and friendly presence, that has kept the restaurant a revered spot in this Fairfield neighborhood.

Liana begins most days working solo in the kitchen, spending a few quiet hours on the ritual of her handmade ravioli and gnocchi. As dinner service begins, and head chef Chris Brant takes over the kitchen, DeMeglio shifts to the dining room, where she can be found greeting customers, many of whom she knows by name. As a result, many of her regulars consider the restaurant an extension of their own dining rooms. When Liana is not in the restaurant, chances are her husband, Tony, who also makes the restaurant's soups and maintains its Italian wine list, will be there.

Sitting down to a meal at Liana's Trattoria begins with the familiar rituals of warm bread and olive oil. The Pasta Nostra connection continues, as a shallow dish of Chef

Bruno's olive oil graces each table, paired with warm crusty Italian bread from nearby Billy's Bakery. A modest menu—a short list of antipasti, pasta, and *secondi,* or classic Italian entrees—has remained largely unchanged for the past twelve years. These classic dishes, Italian home cooking at its finest, are at times rustic and perfectly sourced, like the *Polpettone al Mattone,* a deboned and pan-seared organic baby chicken served over white beans and escarole. At other times, they are elegant and perfectly executed, such as the popular zucchini rollatini antipasto, a trio of thin zucchini slices stuffed with lightly spiced Asiago cheese served over a light tomato-basil sauce. And many are modest while exceeding expectation, like the simply titled eggplant antipasti, an extraordinary take on a singular ingredient, with its sautéed layers of eggplant alternating with slivers of house-made mozzarella and "Donata's special light tomato sauce."

Those qualities coalesce in the house-made pasta such as the Ravioli del Giorno and DeMeglio's inimitable Gnocchi di Liana, the latter earning her the most raucous following among gourmands and fellow chefs, who often imitate but can rarely duplicate her deft touch. Served in three preparations—sage butter, Bolognese, and creamy Gorgonzola—the gnocchi benefit from beginning with East Haven's Calabro ricotta cheese and, of course, decades of practice.

GNOCCHI DI LIANA

RICOTTA GNOCCHI

(SERVES 4)

1 pound ricotta (the very best quality)

1 egg

¾ cup grated Parmigiano Reggiano cheese

3 tablespoons plus ½ teaspoon salt, divided

1 cup all-purpose flour, divided, plus additional
    as needed

Drain ricotta of any excess water by placing it in a sieve or cheese cloth over a bowl. Let drain for at least one hour in the refrigerator.

In a mixing bowl, combine the ricotta, egg, cheese, ½ teaspoon of salt, and ¾ cup of the flour. Mix well. If the dough is too soft, add some more of the remaining ¼ cup of flour. Continue mixing until you get a soft but manageable dough.

Transfer the dough to a large floured cutting board and cut it into four equal pieces. Using your hands, roll each piece into a rope ¾ inch in diameter. Cut the rope into ¾-inch-long pieces. Sprinkle with more flour if they become sticky.

Bring 6 quarts of water to a boil and add 3 table-spoons of salt to the water and then add half of the gnocchi. When they start floating, remove them with a slotted spoon to a serving dish. Repeat with the remaining gnocchi and top them with your favorite sauce. *Buon appetito!*

MATCH RESTAURANT

98 WASHINGTON STREET
SOUTH NORWALK, CT 06854
(203) 852-1088
MATCHSONO.COM
EXECUTIVE CHEF/CO-OWNER: MATT STORCH
CO-OWNER: SCOTT BECK

Synonymous with South Norwalk's thriving restaurant scene, Match Restaurant has been a fixture on Washington Street since opening in 1999. Executive Chef Matt Storch's playful and global approach to its New American menu is inspired by his tireless curiosity and wanderlust, with his love of the Asian flavors inspired by his Vietnamese wife, often pulling rank.

Match dishes are known by their complex and well-balanced layering of flavors, textures, and temperature. A seared wasabi and sesame rubbed tuna, a crunchy and warm exterior giving way to a buttery cool interior, rarely leaves the menu. Another sacred dish, the Carpetbaggers, are warm semolina-fried local bluepoint oysters served back in their respective shells and topped with lightly chilled beef tartare and a dollop of truffle aioli.

The restaurant's burger is so popular that it was given its own night (Thursday). Beginning with a local pasture-raised and grass-fed beef from Roxbury, Storch places the seared beef between a caramelized onion brioche bun with bacon-cheddar sauce and a sweet-and-sour onion jam made from caramelized onions and balsamic vinegar.

It isn't one dish or region that defines the restaurant's approach, but a creative menu filled with carefully constructed dishes and ambitious layering of spices, textures and ingredients. This style is in part created and defined by Matt Storch, chef and partner, who joined the venture shortly after founding partner Scott Beck opened the restaurant in 1999. Storch's passion for cooking began in early in high school, which led him to intern with Todd English's restaurants before and after he graduated from the Culinary Institute of America. Storch and his team at Match have created a restaurant that sits squarely in the epicenter of South Norwalk's dining scene, attracting a discerning and convivial crowd of food lovers.

A dish anchored around tuna with layers of sweet and salty flavors is a perfect representation of Match and its guru, Chef Storch.

Tuna Tartare "Cracker"

Purchase a beautiful piece of tuna from a trusted fishmonger.

(SERVES 4 AS AN APPETIZER)

½ pound tuna
½ cup soy sauce
½ cup maple syrup
1 (6-ounce) pizza dough
2 tablespoons olive oil
½ cup caramelized onions
2 tablespoons capers
2 tablespoons pine nuts
2 tablespoons golden raisins
2 avocados
2 lemons
Salt and pepper to taste
¼ pound ginger, peeled and chopped
1 bunch scallion, chopped
¼ bunch parsley, chopped
2 passion fruits, cut open and yellow flesh removed
    1 tablespoon sesame oil
1–2 tablespoons Sriracha sauce
2 bunches mâche, cleaned
2 tablespoons ginger dressing (see note)

Dice the tuna in very small cubes and place it in the refrigerator.

Place the soy sauce and maple syrup in a saucepan and reduce by half (be careful: this combination acts like milk; when it comes up in temperature, it will boil over the side of the pot).

Preheat a pizza stone to 500°F in the oven. Roll out the pizza dough, brush it with a touch of olive oil, and cover with caramelized onions, capers, pine nuts, and raisins.

Place the pizza in the oven, watch closely, and cook until golden brown. Remove from oven and cut into four squares.

Place the avocado and the juice from the lemons into a blender and puree until smooth; add a touch of salt and black pepper. If the avocado does not puree all the way, add a touch of water.

Remove the tuna from the fridge and mix it with olive oil, sweet soy-syrup mixture, chopped ginger, chopped scallion, chopped parsley, salt, pepper, passion fruit, sesame oil, and 1 tablespoon of Sriracha (or 2 if you like yours spicy).

Take two spoons and make large quenelles, or oval-shaped dumplings, of the tartare and place it on top of each of the pizza "crackers." Top with a dollop of avocado cream. Plate each cracker with a small mâche salad dressed with your favorite ginger vinaigrette.

Note: To make your own ginger dressing take ginger, soy, 10 percent oil, rice vinegar, and mirin, and puree in a blender.

THE CHELSEA

The Chelsea has enjoyed an instant following since its relatively recent 2012 debut, thanks in large part to a familiar and accomplished trio of owners responsible for creating many nearby restaurants: Scott Beck, co-owner of Match (page 110) and The Loft in South Norwalk, and Tavern in Monroe; Matt Storch, chef and co-owner of Match in South Norwalk; and Kevin McHugh, co-owner of Grey Goose in Southport and Spotted Horse in Westport.

Beyond the obvious street cred, its cozy design, and globally inspired menu long on pub classics (it was named after the London neighborhood that launched the gastropub), it has a perceptive sense of the Fairfield County appetite. Think bar food with a case of wanderlust. Calamari meets General Tso's chicken in a fried calamari dish, a Mexican salad with a Greek identity crisis in the case of an avocado-glazed wedge of iceberg topped with beef-filled spanakopita, and lots of Asian influence from a *banh mi* sandwich to a classic noodle bowl.

The Chelsea may look and feel like its upscale restaurant brethren, but leave the formal cruise wear at home. The new kid on the block has a much more relaxed and decidedly whimsical take on many dishes we know, some we love, and several we should get to know better. The Chelsea is located at 12 Unquowa Place, Fairfield, CT 06824; (203) 254-8200; thechelseaff.com.

Norwalk is Connecticut's largest producer of oysters thanks to the hard work of three generations of oystermen and oysterwomen that make up Norm Bloom and Sons. The family business has been in operation since the 1970s, harvesting up to two hundred bushels of oysters each day from the deck of their boat, the *Grace P. Lowndes,* docked in Norwalk Harbor.

Just as the weather dictates the bounty of land for farmers, the quality of the water and cleanliness of the harbors acutely affect the oyster business. Just a few miles from Norwalk Harbor lie the oyster beds, the source of a year-round harvest. Once hauled from the beds, the oysters are taken back to the company's chilled chipping room where they are evaluated for readiness and bagged for delivery.

The Norm Bloom and Sons' celebrated Copps Island oyster can be found on menus across Fairfield County, as well across the country, having helped make New England's bluepoint oysters a household name.

Matsu Sushi

33 Jessup Road
Westport, CT 06880
(203) 341-9662
MATSUSUSHI.NET
Owner: Paul Teoh
Executive Chef/Owner: Michael Cao

Location, location, location. The Japanese restaurant Matsu Sushi benefits from a location in the heart of downtown Westport and a family-friendly and dedicated owner and chef. Situated near the Saugatuck River, Matsu Sushi is adjacent to the town's busy downtown shopping district, making it a prime target for lunch and dinner.

The partnership that formed Matsu Sushi started in upstate New York when Japanese chef Michael Cao met Paul Teoh, an émigré from Malaysia. Teoh, with an accounting and management background, runs the front of the house with his wife,

Pauline, while Cao is focused on the sushi bar. Open for nearly a decade, Matsu Sushi has always focused on impeccably fresh fish for its sushi and has evolved to serve its younger customers with a hibachi menu and sushi-making classes for kids.

The restaurant, a former theater, has soaring floor-to-ceiling windows separating a main dining room from an outdoor patio, an excellent vantage point for the nearby Saugatuck River. A central bar is the restaurant's obvious focal point, and the heart of this family-friendly Westport sushi bar.

There are many sushi spots in Fairfield County, but Matsu stands out in its community-minded participation and focus.

The Ruby Angel and Salmon Confetti Salad are two popular Matsu Sushi dishes pulling in familiar textures such as pasta and a vegetable salad, finished with a strong Asian influence of flavors such as sesame and yuzu.

RUBY ANGEL

(SERVES 1)

8 ounces fresh tuna

6 ounces capellini

For the sauce:

1 teaspoon sesame oil

2 teaspoons grapeseed oil

1 teaspoon soy sauce

1 teaspoon Sriracha sauce

Slice the tuna into strips.

Put capellini in rapidly boiling water, stir occasionally, and cooked, uncovered, for 3 minutes.

Drain pasta and plunge it into ice water for 5 minutes.

To make the sauce: Mix all ingredients together thoroughly.

To serve: Drain the pasta and put into a bowl, add the fresh tuna, and sauce.

Salmon Confetti Salad

(SERVES 1)

1 tablespoon black pepper
6 ounces fresh salmon
1 ounce yellow squash, thinly sliced
1 ounce green squash, thinly sliced
1 ounce turnip (radish), thinly sliced
1 ounce beets, thinly sliced
3 tablespoon yuzu juice (Asian citrus fruit; or
     substitute any citrus)

Apply black pepper to the whole piece of fresh salmon. Lightly pan-sear the salmon on all sides in a lightly oiled pan until cooked to your preferred doneness.

Dip the salmon into ice water for 2 minutes. Take it out, pat dry with a paper towel, and cut it into slices ⅜-inch thick.

Dip the squash, turnip, and beets into ice water for 5 minutes. Drain and dry them with paper towel.

To serve: Place the cut salmon on a large plate, top with squash, turnip, and beets. Pour the yuzu juice evenly over them and serve.

MICHELE'S PIES

666 MAIN AVENUE
NORWALK, CT 06851
(203) 354-7144

180 POST ROAD EAST
WESTPORT, CT 06880
(203) 349-5312
MICHELESPIES.COM
OWNER/CHEF: MICHELE ALBANO

There are few who can argue the transportive powers of a freshly baked pie. The aroma of butter, sugar, and warm fruit emanating from an oven is inextricably tied to home and hearth, holidays and family. Michele Albano has established her growing pie-making empire, Michele's Pies, based on the simple and homespun pies she learned to make from her grandmother.

Drawn by what she explains is "a lost art, an old-fashioned dessert," Michele bases her pies on a decades-old piecrust recipe. Learning early on that simpler is better, each of her pie recipes relies on a few quality ingredients, paired with fresh and seasonal fruit. As a result, Michele's Pies are a sweet reflection of the Connecticut seasons. Rhubarb, blueberry, and peach pies in the summer give way to pumpkin, apple, and pear in the fall, with nuts, cream, and sweet potatoes in the winter, and so on.

Her busiest season begins in September and October, when Michele and her staff turn a truckload of pumpkins from Jones Family Farm in Shelton into four thousand pounds of pumpkin puree to meet the holiday demand for pies of all shapes and sizes. Much of the pumpkin is then frozen to meet the demand for countless pumpkin-pie iterations, ranging from a maple pumpkin with pecan streusel, an award-winning pumpkin chiffon, to her most famous and the subject of a Food Network Bobby Flay "throwdown": her Thanksgiving pumpkin pie.

In addition to being a baker and cafe owner, Michele also lays claim to the title of author and champion with two cookbooks under her belt, dozens of National Pie Championship awards, and numerous TV appearances.

A Connecticut native, Michele got her start in Vermont at farmers' markets, honing her technique and her pie recipes. Experience trumped formal culinary school education, and her diligence netted her the first of many National Pie Championship titles for her chocolate pecan bourbon pie. Michele was able to open her first cafe in Norwalk, closer to home. An appearance on *Good Morning America* led to *Throwdown! with Bobby Flay,* and as they say, the rest is history.

APPLE RASPBERRY CRUMB PIE

(MAKES ONE 9-INCH PIE)

Michele's apple-raspberry crumb pie is ideally prepared in late summer, when raspberries are at their peak in Connecticut. The combination of the fruit is naturally sweet, so little additional sugar is necessary. And making your own piecrust isn't mandatory, but it is an ideal match for the at-peak, seasonal fruit.

For the piecrust:

2 cups unbleached all-purpose flour, plus additional
    for rolling
1 teaspoon salt
¾ cup plus 2 tablespoons Crisco, cold
5 tablespoons ice-cold water
⅛ cup heavy cream

For the apple raspberry filling:

1 cup sugar
3 tablespoons unbleached all-purpose flour
1 tablespoons ground cinnamon
Dash of nutmeg
6 medium apples, peeled, cored, and cut into
    ½-inch chunks
2 cups fresh raspberries, washed and dried

For the cinnamon-sugar crumb topping:

½ cup unbleached all-purpose flour
⅓ cup firmly packed brown sugar
1 teaspoon ground cinnamon
¼ teaspoon salt
5 tablespoons unsalted butter, cold and cut into
    ¼-inch cubes

To make the piecrust: In a medium bowl, mix together the flour and salt, then add the Crisco. Using your hands, mix in a fingertip fashion until the dough becomes pea-size pieces. Add the ice cold water, 1 tablespoon at a time, and gently incorporate the water into the flour mixture. You may have to use an extra tablespoon of water, or one less, depending on how the flour takes in the water based on the humidity level in the kitchen. You will know you have added the right amount of water when the dough forms a ball that will hold itself together.

Wrap the ball of dough in plastic wrap and refrigerate for at least 30 minutes.

Divide the dough in half. For this pie, you will only need half of the dough. Reserve the other half for future use in your refrigerator or freezer.

On a floured surface, roll out half of the dough until it forms a 10-inch circle. Fold the circle in half, place it in the pie plate, and crimp the edges. Brush heavy cream around the edges of the pie shell and set aside.

To make the filling: Preheat oven to 425°F.

In a small bowl, whisk together the sugar, flour, cinnamon, and nutmeg. In a medium bowl, combined the apples and raspberries. Sprinkle the dry mixture over the apple-raspberry mixture and gently toss until well combined.

Place the apple raspberry mixture into the crimped pie shell. Set aside while you make the cinnamon-sugar crumb topping.

To make crumb topping: In a medium bowl, mix together the flour, brown sugar, cinnamon, and salt. Using a pastry blender, incorporate the butter by cutting it into the flour mixture until the butter is small, pea-size pieces.

Sprinkle this crumb topping on top of the apple raspberry filling.

Place the pie on a baking sheet lined with parchment paper, and set it on the middle rack of the oven and cook at 425°F for 15 minutes. Turn the temperature down to 375°F and continue to bake for another 35–40 minutes or until the pie is golden brown and juices bubbling. The apples should also be tender; check by inserting a cake tester or knife into the pie.

Remove the pie from the oven and transfer to a wire cooling rack. Allow the pie to cool and set for at least 1½ hours.

Food trucks in Fairfield County—a small but growing number of restaurants on wheels—are a diverse bunch.

The tiniest of the fleet, Chez Lenard (chezlenard.com), is also one of the oldest. The Ridgefield hot dog cart pre-dated the food-truck trend with its presence on the town's Main Street since 1978. Chez Lenard has changed hands a few times, but it still serves up specialties such as Le Hot Dog Epicie Garniture Suisse, a hot dog with spicy horse-radish cheese fondue of white wine and kirsch.

In Norwalk, Short and Sweet Cupcake Truck (shortandsweetcupcakes.ca) is the baking brainchild of sixteen-year-old twins Kate and Gavin Nelson. The young and driven duo manages their entire operation from the truck's fully mobile kitchen with classic flavors of vanilla, chocolate, red velvet, and mint chocolate.

Skinny Pines Pizza (skinnypines.com), based in Easton, is a familiar face from the Westport and New Canaan farmers' markets, which is also the source for most of their ingredients. Known for its sustainable practices, the wood-fired mobile brick oven is used most often for 8-inch Neapolitan-inspired pizzas.

For the lunch crowd, the El Charrito taco truck (page 76) in Stamford draws a steady stream of tie-wearing professionals. Their tacos are a Stamford icon. Snappy Dawg (snappydawgs.com) in Bridgeport has its own own comfort food–loving cult followers, while Christophe's Crepe Truck (646-596-6879) in Fairfield embraces its own take on comfort food, with a decidedly upscale, Gallic twist.

The newest to make it onto the mobile scene are also the most celebrated. Melt Mobile (meltmobilect .com) in Stamford is a grilled cheese truck that had some help in its launch from Bobby Flay. It draws a diverse crowd with its warm and crispy melted cheese creations. Maddy's Food Truck (maddysfoodtruck.com) has hit the Stamford streets with her creative creole dishes and offers a combination of classic American and family-inspired Haitian recipes.

Lobster Craft (lobstercraft.com), based in Norwalk, brings several versions of the warm buttered lobster roll to the masses "from boat to bun." Also in Norwalk and combining two of America's classic beach foods, Cowabunga Food Truck (cowabungafoodtruck.com) "surfs" around Norwalk cooking up burgers, fries, and soft-serve ice cream.

It's impossible to miss The Local Meatball (thelocalmeatball.com) inhabiting a bright red Smart Car hitched to a kitchen cart around the streets of Fairfield. Their "serious" meatballs are available as sliders, grinders, or "just da balls."

Napa & Co.

75 Broad Street
Stamford, CT 06901
(203) 353-3319
NAPAANDCOMPANY.COM
Co-Owners: Mary Schaffer and Charles Morgan

The art of food and wine pairing is the culinary métier of Napa & Co., the downtown Stamford restaurant in business since 2006. Owned by sommelier Mary Schaffer and her husband, Charles Morgan, the restaurant takes an even-handed approach to its food and wine program, devoting equal amounts of energy to sourcing and producing its own wine, selecting wine from singular growing regions around the country, and preparing and presenting a complementary seasonal American menu.

Named for the California region known as the heart of our country's finest wine vineyards as well as a robust network of farms and artisan products, Napa & Co. looks to its farm-centric food and oenophile focus to inform its menu and dining spaces. An airy main dining space with tall windows faces the busy streets of Stamford and evokes a market-like feel while a cozier space referred to as the Wine Closet is the setting for private wine dinners and events.

Napa has been the staging ground for several of Fairfield County's most critically acclaimed chefs, from Bill Taibe of leFarm (page 102) and The Whelk (page 184), to Arik Bensimon of The Spread, and most recently, to Leonardo Marino, who took over the reins of its kitchen in the summer of 2012 (he recently departed the restaurant). Marino came to Napa & Co. with solid time spent at several of New York City's revered French outposts such as Le Bernardin and Bouley, bringing his own focus to what he describes as "natural flavors and excellent ingredients." His deft touch with fish (a whisper of Le

Bernardin) and a hearty embrace of his Italian heritage feature prominently on the Napa & Co. menu.

At any moment during the year, the menu is a snapshot of that particular seasonal moment in time, with constant consideration of how mutual compositions and pairings of food and wine can elevate an already stellar dish and bottle of wine.

Heirloom Tomato Salad, Burrata, Grilled Bread & White Balsamic Vinegar Gelée

(SERVES 1)

For the gelée:

1 sheet gelatin

4 tablespoons cold water

¾ cup plus 4 tablespoons good-quality white balsamic vinegar

For the salad:

⅓ cup assorted heirloom tomatoes, cut into wedges, and cherry tomatoes, cut in half

¼ cup rustic Italian bread, torn, seasoned with extra-virgin olive oil, salt, pepper, and lightly grilled

½ cup burrata, cut into 5 pieces

For the garnish:

Maldon sea salt and black pepper to taste

Extra-virgin olive oil, preferably Frantoia

White balsamic gelée

Fresh green and opal basil, julienned

To make the gelée: Bloom the gelatin in cold water to soften the sheet to ensure a smooth texture. To bloom, sprinkle the powdered gelatin with cold water and let it sit for a few minutes before preparing as written.

Bring the vinegar to a boil and remove from heat. Place the softened sheet of gelatin into the hot vinegar and whisk well. Place into a container and refrigerate until the mixture forms a gel. Reserve for serving.

To make the salad: Arrange the tomatoes on a rimless round plate while the bread is being grilled.

To grill the bread: Brush the bread with olive oil and place on a medium heat grill until lightly charred and crispy on each side.

Randomly place the bread in and around the tomatoes, then place the burrata in the remaining space. Season with Maldon sea salt and black pepper from the mill, drizzle aggressively with olive oil, and gently place the gelée on the tomatoes.

Garnish with green and opal basil julienne.

Juice bars and cafes have been cropping up with increasing speed across Fairfield County, as its residents embrace juicing's claims of healing and health.

Founded in 2010, Green & Tonic's cold pressed juices and superfood smoothies form the backbone of a nutrient dense menu. The brainchild of two chefs, a nutritionist, a fitness expert, and a mom, Green & Tonic's approach—to create an authentic, wholesome, full and healthy life—has now expanded to three locations across Fairfield County.

Kaia Cafe is an organic juice bar with freshly squeezed juices, boosts, and smoothies aimed at serving its yoga-loving clientele. In addition to juices, 20 organic teas are offered by the cup or pot, as are coffee-based beverages with their excellent homemade almond milk.

The Stand Juice Company has made their mark with a popular three- and five-day detoxifying juice cleanse. One of their greenest juices is called "The Nasty," a seriously green juice of greens, garlic, ginger, and cayenne.

The raw vegan cafe Catch a Healthy Habit in Fairfield is the elder statesman of the Fairfield County juice community. The smoothie and juice menu dominates the cafe's menu, many using a blend including the cafe's

homemade almond milk and a variety of organic vegetables and fruit. The cafe also offers intrepid juicers a five-day liquid cleanse throughout the year.

Embody Fitness & Gourmet's approach is equal parts body and mind. Their "Blend Bar," or smoothie offerings, as well as their Juice Bar menu lists calorie and protein information alongside a list of ingredients. "Vitalizers" are meant to nourish as well as invigorate, including popular tea-based beverages such as the Surge, a blend of green tea, lemon, agave and fresh mint.

Green & Tonic
1098 Boston Post Road, Darien; (203) 656-1036
7 Strickland Road, Cos Cob; (203) 869-1376
85 Railroad Avenue, Greenwich; (203) 622-1479
greenandtonic.com

Kaia Cafe
1200 Post Road East, Westport; (203) 532-0660
328 Pemberwick Road, Greenwich; (203) 532-0660
kaiayoga.com

The Stand Juice Company
31 Wall Street, Norwalk; (203) 956-5670
87 Mill Plain Road, Fairfield; (203) 873-0414
thestandjuice.com

Catch a Healthy Habit
Embody Fitness Gourmet
54 Riverside Avenue, Westport; (203) 557-4144
catchahealthyhabit.com

Embody Fitness
545 Riverside Ave, Westport; (203) 557-4144
@ Equinox Fitness Club of Darien, 72 Heights Road, Darien; (203) 202-2760

@ YMCA of Darien, 2420 Boston Post Road. (US 1), Darien; (203) 599-0007
embodyfitnessgourmet.com

NICHOLAS ROBERTS GOURMET BISTRO

75 MAIN STREET
NORWALK, CT 06851
(203) 299-0035
NICHOLASROBERTSBISTRO.COM
CHEF/OWNER: ROBERT TROILO

Chef Robert "Rob" Troilo brings both a sense of humor and cool sophistication to his laid-back bistro, Nicholas Roberts Gourmet Bistro, or NRGB, in Norwalk. A creative family affair, NRGB is a collaboration with his father and frequent host, Nicholas, and brother Peter, who manages their sister store, Nicholas Roberts Fine Wines. Leading the charge of "enriching others' lives through food and wine," it is Rob who is the creative core of the twenty-five-seat Norwalk bistro.

A graduate of the French Culinary Institute, Chef Troilo spent time at the fine-

dining outpost Homestead Inn, in Greenwich, and several of Norwalk's best restaurants before embarking on his own catering and restaurant business. Although it has become a popular spot over the years, its nondescript Norwalk location and BYOB and no-reservations policies still manage to make it feel like a well-kept secret speakeasy.

Crossing through the thick velvet curtains just and over the threshold the Bistro's strip-mall entrance is an open kitchen and dining room, crowned by an extensive hand-drawn chalkboard menu. An informal bistro space during the day, dim lighting and candlelight transform the space for the evening crowd, who embrace dinner's modest prices and BYOB policy.

An award-winning lobster bisque, Maker's Mark mac and cheese, and hanger steak frites are among Chef Troilo's signature dishes in the evenings, with changing weekly specials depending on what the chef has uncovered at the farmers' markets. During the morning rush, regulars flock daily for hearty breakfast burritos paired with local Zumbach's coffee. Brunch, that most important of weekend meals, is the most coveted of all the Nicholas Roberts meals with an unforgettable fried egg corn tortilla served with short rib, tomato, and black beans, and brioche french toast.

The unsung hero of NRGB is lunch. The sandwiches, such as the lobster roll, offers glimpses of the inventive and energetic flavors that dinner affords and that breakfast can only dream of.

LOBSTER ROLLS WITH SAFFRON BUTTER

(SERVES 6)

1 fennel bulb, roughly chopped

2 medium carrots, peeled and roughly chopped

2 onions, peeled and roughly chopped

2 cups dry white wine

6 tarragon sprigs

6 parsley sprigs

2 tablespoons peppercorns

2 lemons, cut in half

3 (2-pound) lobsters

6 thin slices prosciutto (preferably La Quercia Prosciutto Americano)

1 teaspoon saffron threads

¼ cup carrots, diced

3 tablespoons shallots, diced

¼ cup celery, diced

2 ounces clarified butter

Salt and pepper to taste

1 tablespoon ¼-inch-long fennel fronds

6 brioche hamburger rolls

6 leaves of Bibb lettuce

6 ripe tomato slices

Extra-virgin olive oil

Preheat the oven to 350°F.

Put the roughly chopped fennel, carrots, and onion, along with the wine, tarragon, parsley, and peppercorns in a pot large enough to hold the lobsters. Squeeze the lemon juice into the pot, add the lemon halves, and fill with enough water so that the lobsters will be completely submerged when added. Salt the water to the point that it tastes like the ocean. Place the pot on the stove and bring the water to a rapid boil.

To produce the most tender lobsters, it is important that the pot is large enough to hold enough water so that once the lobsters are added the water will not lose its boil or will return to a boil quickly. If the pot or the range is not sufficient enough to maintain the boil or bring it back quickly, you should cook the lobsters one at a time.

Add the lobsters to the boiling water and cook for 7 minutes.

In the meantime place the prosciutto on a baking sheet and bake until crisp, about 5 minutes.

When the 7 minutes are up promptly remove the lobsters from the boiling water with a pair of tongs and submerge them in a bucket filled with cold water and ice. Once the lobsters are cooled, crack the shells and remove all the meat in the tail, arms, and claws. Cut the tail meat in half lengthwise and trim off the rubbery tips of the claws.

Place the saffron threads, diced vegetables, and butter in a sauté pan. Bring to a simmer, reduce the heat to low, and let simmer for 2 minutes. Add the lobster to the pan, season with salt and pepper, and stir to coat the lobster. Toss in the fennel fronds.

Slice the hamburger rolls in half and toast in a 350°F oven until slightly golden. Remove the rolls from the oven and place a slice of prosciutto on the bottom of each roll. Divide the lobster meat evenly atop each piece of prosciutto, giving each roll one claw, half a tail and the meat of one arm. Drizzle the lobster with the butter remaining in the pan. Place the lettuce and tomato on top of the lobster. Season with salt and pepper and drizzle with a touch of extra-virgin olive oil.

PACI

96 STATION STREET
SOUTHPORT, CT 06490
(203) 259-9600
PACIRESTAURANT.COM
CHEF/OWNER: DONNA & ROBERT J. PATCHEN

Donna and Robert Patchen are the owners of Paci, a seventeen-year-old Italian restaurant in the gentrified two-hundred-year-old Southport train depot. Robert Patchen is a self-taught chef whose unusually keen palate belies a penchant for simple and classic ingredients. His partner and wife, Donna, is equally smitten by ingredients as well as an appreciation for fine wine. This means Paci begins and ends with perfect seasonal ingredients, with their chosen Italian approach that is not locked into any particular region or style.

Dishes such as burrata and house-made pastas rotate with the seasons and their accompanying ingredients. Carefully sourced quality cuts of meat speak to Paci's single-minded approach, a celebration of a central ingredient with a disdain for saucing and layering.

During the original renovation of the early nineteenth-century structure, receipts for hay bales and onions were uncovered, confirming its original commercial purpose as a warehouse for foodstuff and livestock. An original wooden sliding door and a soaring lofted interior are the architectural harbingers of its agrarian merchant roots.

The space may have working-class roots, but its incarnation into a fine dining destination is anything but rustic. Its most dramatic and signature design element is a large railway station clock projected onto the wall of the dining room. A second level above half the building's footprint has additional seating for busy weekend nights, and underneath is a modest yet undeniably cozy bar.

VITELLO MILANESE

VEAL MILANESE

(SERVES 4–6)

2 pounds top round veal cutlets, about 4–6 veal cutlets
1 loaf ciabatta bread
1 cup flour
3 large eggs
Extra-virgin olive oil
Vine-ripe cherry tomatoes
Minced garlic
Fresh chopped basil

Lightly pound the veal cutlets, but not too thin.

Slice the ciabatta bread and bake it in a low oven until it is dried out, but be careful not to brown.

Grind bread to a medium crumb consistency.

Dredge the pounded veal in flour, then dip into the egg, then the bread crumbs. Lightly press the crumbs into the veal so they cling to the meat.

Heat a large frying pan with enough oil to cover the bottom of the pan on medium-high heat. Do not let oil smoke.

Place breaded veal gently in pan and brown veal on each side, about 6–8 minutes total time per cutlet depending on its size.

Remove finished veal from pan and place on paper towels to absorb excess oil before garnishing.

Garnish with chopped tomatoes tossed with oil, garlic, and basil.

Strawberry Shortcake

(SERVES 6)

For the shortcakes:

2 cups pastry flour

2 teaspoons baking powder

½ pint toasted almonds, baked 9 minutes
   and pulsed to medium-fine consistency

½ cup granulated sugar

¼ teaspoon salt

1 egg

1 egg yolk

⅓ cup heavy cream

¼ teaspoon vanilla

¼ pound (1 stick) unsalted butter, cut into
   small pieces

For the strawberry mixture:

2 pints fresh strawberries

¼ teaspoon salt

2 teaspoons granulated sugar

For the whipped cream mixture:

1 pint heavy cream

1 teaspoon vanilla

3 teaspoons granulated sugar

Fresh mint for garnish

To make the shortcakes: Combine flour, baking powder, ground toasted almonds, sugar, and salt in a bowl. Combine egg, egg yolk, cream, and vanilla in another bowl.

With fork work butter into the flour mixture and then combine with the egg mixture. Combine together to form a ball; you will need to use your hands. Divide into six equal-size, roughly formed balls.

Line a sheet pan with parchment paper. Place balls on paper, sprinkle with sugar, and place in a convection oven (or preheated 425°F oven) for 12–14 minutes or until golden brown. Cool.

To make the strawberry mixture: Slice strawberries and combine with salt and sugar. Set aside.

To make the whipped cream: Combine cream, vanilla, and sugar. Whip until stiff peaks form.

To serve: Cut shortcakes horizontally in half or thirds. Layer whipped cream, strawberries, and shortcake. Top with a dollop of whipped cream and fresh mint.

Metro North trains are a daily ritual and lifeline to many Fairfield County communities who depend on them for work and play. For some lucky commuters, there are several eateries quite literally on the platform, jockeying for position and making the drudgery of commuting literally palatable.

Situated on the northbound side of the Fairfield train station, Nauti Dolphin (1 Carter Henry Drive, Fairfield; 203-256-1877) serves up unpretentious New York–inspired slices and pies for commuters. A sliver of a space, just big enough for a counter, prep space, and a wall of gas-powered ovens, means that both takeout and delivery rule for this neighborhood favorite.

In Fairfield's enclave of Southport, the farm-to-table gem of Paci (page 130) is the swankiest of the train set. This upscale Italian restaurant is situated inside Southport's former train station, transformed into one of its most beautiful dining rooms.

At the Greens Farms Station, Steam Coffee Bar (2 Post Office Lane, Westport; http://steamcoffeebar.com) celebrates the anything but humble coffee bean and brews all varieties of Raus Coffee into espresso drinks thanks to its La Marzocco machines.

The Whistle Stop Bakery in the quiet town of Ridgefield (20 Portland Avenue; whistlestopbakery.com) is a sleepy commuter's dream, with hot coffee and immense scones and baked goods cooked daily. A familiar face at area farmers' markets, it has cornered the weekend-treat market with their Sunday Sticky Buns.

Located inside the Bethel train station, Daily Fare (13 Durant Avenue, Bethel; dailyfare.net) catches commuters coming and going with breakfast and catering. Mornings are devoted to freshly baked granola bars and scones and paired with locally roasted coffee sourced from fellow Bethel business Redding Roasters.

THE SCHOOLHOUSE AT CANNONDALE

34 CANNON ROAD
WILTON, CT 06897
(203) 834-9816
SCHOOLHOUSEATCANNONDALE.COM
CHEF/OWNER: TIM LABANT

The Schoolhouse at Cannondale, a quaint one-room schoolhouse situated along the banks of the Norwalk River, is the embodiment of the quintessential New England restaurant. Located in Wilton, its single building and flagstone terrace are nestled alongside a series of small antique buildings, including the Cannondale train station.

Its storied four walls were once an object of affection for former owner and vaudeville star June Havoc, younger sister of Gypsy Rose Lee. It caught the attention of passionate locavore and Wilton native, Chef/Owner Tim LaBant when it came up for lease in 2006. In his able hands, the building's current incarnation stands as a locus for one of Fairfield County's most memorable farm-to-table dining experiences, sited conveniently near many of Fairfield County's farms.

If the white clapboard exterior is rustic school charm, the interior is scholarly elegance, outfitted with walls of chocolate brown, houndstooth banquettes, and clean, white architectural details. This interior refinement matches a carefully edited selection of three courses that changes frequently. Chef LaBant frequently offers special tasting menus and events, often teaming up with nearby farms such as Millstone Farm and Ambler Farm for farm dinners and fund-raisers. These agricultural partners highlight the chef's embrace of and deft touch with vegetables.

Chef LaBant attended culinary school after a stint in corporate America. He worked with Chef Ming Tsai and honed his skills in French cuisine while working at the Boston's four-star L'Espalier Restaurant.

The Schoolhouse at Cannondale's tiny footprint translates into an intimate setting, a perfect location for the nuanced layering of flavors and textures that is LaBant's signature. Carefully selected vegetables such as hen-of-the-woods mushrooms and fresh herbs compete for attention with locally sourced proteins such as squab.

ROASTED SQUAB WITH DUCK CONFIT, SUNCHOKE PUREE & PICKLED BEECH MUSHROOMS

(SERVES 6)

For the Squab

3 (1-pound) squab
4–6 tablespoons salt
6 tablespoons duckfat

Clean and break down the squab: Remove the innards, wings at the elbow joint, legs, and head or neck (if no head); remove the tail half of the backbone if desired. Reserve neck, wings, legs, and back, if desired, for making stock another day.

Lightly salt the breast cage and legs and refrigerate at least 4 hours before cooking.

Preheat the oven to 425°F.

Heat a heavy, ovenproof pan on high heat, add a little duck fat to the pan. When first wisps of smoke begin on edges of pan, gently place the squab, breast side down, in the pan. Brown the entire breast, which should take about 5 minutes. When the squab is a deep golden brown, flip it breast side up and put the entire pan into a 425°F oven for 12 minutes.

Remove the squab, let it rest for 10 minutes, and then carve it.

DUCK CONFIT

(SERVES 6)

For the herb salt:

½ cup kosher salt
1 tablespoon herbes de Provence

For the duck

6 duck legs, excess fat trimmed and reserved
fresh chopped herbs, such as thyme, sage

Day one: To make herb salt, blend salt and herbes de Provence in food processor for 15 seconds. Season the duck legs with herb salt, cover, and refrigerate overnight.

Day two: Rinse duck legs in water and then dry with paper towels.

Preheat oven to 300°F.

Heat enough duck fat from the trimmed legs to submerge the legs in an ovenproof pot. Place the duck legs in fat and bring the pot to a simmer. As soon as the duck simmers, cover it with a lid and place in the oven for 3 hours.

Take the pot from the oven and remove duck legs from fat. Once the legs are cool enough, pick off all the meat and discard the skin and bones.

Season duck meat with salt to taste and fresh chopped herbs.

Lay out a sheet of aluminum foil and make a pile of shredded duck in a rough but tight log shape on one-quarter of the foil (like you're rolling sushi). Make sure to leave about 2 inches of space on either end and roll it up. Twist and pinch the ends. Refrigerate for at least 6 hours or overnight.

When ready to serve slice off a 1-inch piece of the duck log and sear it in a pan with a little of the reserved duck fat. Be sure to remove the foil before serving!

SUNCHOKE PUREE

(SERVES 6)

1 pound sunchokes, peeled and placed in
    acidulated water
1 bay leaf
2 cloves garlic
1 cup half-and-half
2 tablespoons unsalted butter

Place the sunchokes, bay leaf, and garlic in a pot of water and boil until the sunchokes are tender but not falling apart, about 10–15 minutes. Remove bay leaf and garlic, and strain out the water.

Warm half-and-half and butter in a small saucepan.

Combine sunchokes and warm butter mixture in a powerful blender and blend on high for 2 minutes. Pass through a chinois when complete.

PICKLED BEECH MUSHROOMS

Start this recipe a day in advance.

(SERVES 6)

4 ounces beech mushrooms, cleaned
½ cup sherry vinegar
½ cup water
2½ tablespoons salt

Place the mushrooms in a covered container.

Simmer the sherry vinegar, water, and salt until combined and dissolved and pour it over the mushrooms. Cover the container with a lid and keep it at room temperature for 2 hours, then refrigerate overnight.

SoNo Baking Company & Cafe

101 Water Street
Norwalk, CT 06854
(203) 847-7666

1680 Post Road East at A&J's Farmstand
Westport, CT 06880
(203) 955-1111
SONOBAKING.COM
Owner/Baker: John Barricelli

A deeply ingrained passion for baking is what keeps John Barricelli rising at 3 a.m. every morning after all these years. Barricelli is the owner of SoNo Baking Company, a bakery and cafe in Norwalk and Westport. A former regular on *The Martha Stewart Show* and host of *Everyday Food* on PBS, John Barricelli has become something of a regional celebrity in the world of baking. Since opening in 2005, SoNo Baking Company & Cafe has become a source for artisanal breads, specialty cakes, delicate pastries, as well as savory snacks and sandwiches. It's hard to dine out in Fairfield County without unwittingly biting into a SoNo Baking Company brioche. Family figures prominently for Barricelli. Sunday dinners in Brooklyn with three generations of his Italian family anchor his earliest and fondest memories of food. He is the third generation of his family to bake, a tradition he chronicles through recipes in his second cookbook filled with family recipes and that he shares with his own three children.

From home hearth to an early stint in the kitchen at Brooklyn's River Café, Barricelli found himself at the Culinary Institute of America and subsequent stages in the storied kitchens of Le Bernardin, the Four Seasons, and finally the test kitchen of *The Martha Stewart Show,* which galvanized his approach to baking with its endless and ever-changing list of ingredients at his disposal.

Paired with a boundless curiosity, Barricelli was inspired to strike out on his own, opening SoNo Baking Company in Norwalk.

The SoNo Baking Company's cafe, housed in a 3,600-square-foot former warehouse a stone's throw Norwalk Harbor, is a popular draw for the lively South Norwalk neighborhood. Its original location has an open kitchen and bakery, providing a bird's-eye view of the breads that are baked fresh every morning in an Italian-imported deck oven. Baguette, sourdough, multigrain, focaccia, semolina, and *pain au levain* are in regular rotation. Weekly and seasonal special breads such as challah make regular appearances. Pastries tend to skew Gallic, from his signature tarts, galettes, and pies to his own creations. Its baking aesthetic is markedly French, with influences that span the entirety of Europe.

CARAMEL–APPLE TART

(SERVES 8)

For the dough:

2¼ cups all-purpose flour

2 teaspoons sugar

1 teaspoon coarse salt

1 cup (2 sticks) cold unsalted butter, cut into small pieces

¼ cup ice water

For the caramel pastry cream:

2 large egg yolks

1 tablespoon plus ¼ cup granulated sugar, divided

2 tablespoons cornstarch

⅛ teaspoon coarse salt

1 cup whole milk

¼ teaspoon vinegar

1 teaspoon pure vanilla extract

1½ tablespoons cold unsalted butter, cut into small pieces

For the filling:

4 Granny Smith apples, peeled, cored, and halved. Cut each apple half crosswise (across the short side, perpendicular to the top stem) into ⅛-inch thick slices

6 tablespoons unsalted butter, melted

¼ cup confectioners' sugar

1 cup apricot jam

Special equipment:

8½ x 12-inch rimmed baking sheet

To make the dough: In the bowl of a food processor, combine the flour, sugar, and salt. Add the butter and pulse until the mixture resembles coarse crumbs with visible, chickpea-size bits of butter, about 10 seconds. With the machine running, add the ice water through the feed tube, a little bit at a time until everything is moistened and the dough just begins to clump together, but has not yet formed a ball. You will see unincorporated bits of butter. If the dough is too dry and does not hold together, add a little more water.

Turn the dough out onto a sheet of plastic wrap, shape into a flattened disk, and wrap in the plastic. Chill for at least 1 hour before using.

Tip: To make ice water, combine ¼ cup water and 1 or 2 ice cubes in a bowl and let stand for 5 minutes to chill the water. Remove the ice.

To make the pastry cream: In a medium, heat-proof bowl, whisk together the yolks, 1 tablespoon of the sugar, the cornstarch, salt, and ¼ cup of the milk; set aside.

In a medium saucepan, combine the remaining ¼ cup sugar, 3 tablespoons water, and the vinegar. Bring to a boil over medium-high heat, swirling the pan to dissolve the sugar. Boil until the mixture turns a deep amber color, 5–10 minutes. Remove from the heat, and add the remaining ¾ cup milk. Stand back: The caramel will spit and the milk will boil up. Return the pan to medium heat and stir until the caramel melts and the mixture is smooth.

Whisking constantly, gradually pour the hot caramel-milk into the egg yolk mixture to temper. Set a strainer over the empty saucepan; strain the mixture back into the pan. Bring to a boil over medium heat, whisking constantly. Let boil for 10 seconds (in the center of the pan, not just around the sides), still whisking. The mixture should thicken to a pudding-like consistency. Transfer to the bowl of a standing mixer fitted with the paddle attachment. Beat the cream 2–3 minutes to cool slightly. Beat in the vanilla, then the butter. Beat until cooled, 5–10 more minutes. Press a piece of plastic wrap directly on the surface to prevent a skin from forming, and refrigerate.

On a lightly floured surface, roll the dough to a 14 x 12-inch rectangle, ⅛–¼-inch thick. Roll the dough up around the rolling pin and transfer to an 8½ x 12-inch rimmed baking sheet. Trim the dough, as necessary, to about ¼ inch above the rim of the pan. Crimp the edges. Chill until firm, about 30 minutes.

Set the oven rack in the lower third of the oven. Preheat the oven to 425°F.

Use an offset spatula to spread the caramel pastry cream in the dough, leaving a ½-inch border all around. Push each apple half forward to fan the slices. With one of the long sides of the baking pan facing you, place a fanned apple half on top of the pastry cream, in the upper corner, along one short side of the shell. Continue with another apple half below the first. Continue to arrange three more rows of apple halves until the shell is filled. Brush with the melted butter and sift confectioners' sugar generously over the top.

Bake, rotating the tart about two-thirds of the way through the baking time, until golden brown, 30–45 minutes. Wrap the edges of the crust in aluminum foil if it browns too much. Transfer to a wire rack.

While the tart is still warm, in a small saucepan, warm the apricot jam over low heat until liquid. Strain through a fine strainer. Brush the top of the tart lightly with jam to seal the fruit and give the tart a nice shine. Allow the tart to cool completely.

Cut the tart into eight squares and serve.

SOUTH END

36 PINE STREET
NEW CANAAN, CT 06840
(203) 966-5200
SOUTHENDNEWCANAAN.COM
CHEF/CO-OWNER: NICK MARTSCHENKO
CO-OWNER/GENERAL MANAGER: KEITH SISKIND

New Canaan's South End restaurant is a fitting reflection of its New Canaan environs. A modern American tavern, South End's approach to dining reflects a dedication to seasonality, an integrity toward source, and a design that embraces New Canaan's quaint yet ultimately urbane duality.

In a town with many farm-to-table dining options, co-owner and chef Nick Martschenko distinguishes South End's seasonal approach with an American comfort-food interpretation. Ruffage, South End's version of salads, features the Baby Iceberg Wedge, a modern take on a familiar classic—a quintessential South End interpretation. A smaller-scale variation on the beloved original, the South End version is built around a small wedge of iceberg adorned with bits of lardon, shards of Maytag blue cheese, and cucumber "spaghetti," and finished with buttermilk dressing.

Main courses are familiar and at times hearty, such as Martschenko's signature dish (and the chef's self-professed favorite). House-made tagliatelle is layered in a rich Bolognese, a combination of veal, pork, and beef, finished with rosemary and basil. South End's version of classic bistro dishes such as chicken paillard and steak frites are perennial favorites, with equal emphasis on seafood favorites such as oysters, halibut, and diver scallops.

These proteins tend to anchor the menu but shift personalities with rotating seasonal accompaniments. Spring's ramps and fiddleheads are followed by a rotation of summer's leafy greens, fruits, peas, tomatoes, and so on. They can appear roasted as sides but are just as likely to become memorable and key ingredients in sauces, blended into butters, and emulsified into vinaigrettes.

Chef Nick Martschenko is a graduate of the Culinary Institute of America, and an

alum of some well-known New York City kitchens such as Gramercy Tavern and I Trulli. A prescient mentorship with James Beard award–winning chef Melissa Kelly, a devoted locavore who runs her own full-circle kitchen in Maine, fused his classically trained approach with a deep awareness of the importance of seasonality. His stints in New York and later Connecticut amplified his love of the types of comfort food he enjoys eating as well as serving.

Taking cues from its seasonal comfort-food kitchen, reclaimed barn wood and linen drapes anchor a palette of natural colors and rustic textures. The restaurant's black banquette seating and a handsome bar—a hive of activity—elevate the overtly agrestic with a hint of modernity. Co-owners Nick Martschenko and general manager Keith Siskind have succeeded in creating a quintessential modern American neighborhood tavern—at times both rustic and refined yet ultimately approachable.

Martschenko's barbecued octopus is a southern take on a typically Mediterranean or Spanish dish. The combination of grilled andouille, smoked bread crumbs, and romesco sauce is a playful interpretation of barbecue sauce.

GRILLED OCTOPUS WITH ROMESCO, GRILLED ANDOUILLE, SMOKED BREADCRUMBS & CHARRED OLIVES

(MAKES 8 PORTIONS)

This recipe is a two-step process: First braise the octopus until tender, then marinate and grill the octopus to develop a nice char, providing texture and flavor. This recipe works well with large octopus or baby octopus.

For the octopus:

5 pounds large octopus, cleaned

For the marinade:

3 tablespoons extra virgin olive oil
1 half lemon
1 half orange
1 half lime
A few thyme sprigs

Aromatic braising liquid:

½ bottle dry white wine
2 cups champagne vinegar
1 bulb fennel
2 stalks celery
1 onion
1 orange, halved
2 lemons, halved
2 tablespoons extra virgin olive oil

Sachet of:

2 pieces, Star anise
10 cardamom pods
2 tablespoons toasted fennel seed
3 sprigs thyme
1 bay leaf
2 sprigs tarragon

Put braising liquid and sachet in a large stockpot and cover with water. Bring up to a boil and then slowly simmer for 30 minutes. Strain out aromatics and season the liquid aggressively with salt. Add rinsed octopus and simmer for approximately 45 minutes, until tender.

Combine the ingredients for the marinade. Strain the octopus and add to the marinade.

For the romesco:

2 roasted peppers, peeled and seeded
2 roasted tomatoes
¼ cup toasted almonds
¼ cup toasted hazelnuts
½ lemon zest
2 tablespoons sherry vinegar
¼ cup extra virgin olive oil
1 teaspoon harissa
2–3 slices of crusty bread, coated with olive oil
    and grilled
salt, to taste
freshly ground black pepper, to taste

Put all the ingredients in a food processor and puree until smooth. Season to taste with salt and freshly ground black pepper.

For the burnt olive oil:

1 cup pitted black olives, preferably gaeta
    or kalamata, divided
¼ cup extra virgin olive oil

Slowly cook the olives on a sheet tray in an oven at 250°F for 1 hour or until crispy. (This can also be done in a dehydrator).

Put half of the olives in a food processor and slowly drizzle in the extra virgin olive oil until incorporated. Reserve the other half for finishing the dish.

Putting it all together:

1 tablespoon of extra virgin olive oil
½ teaspoon Espellette seasoning
sea salt, to taste
1 andouille sausage
1 bunch baby arugula

Season the octopus with olive oil, Espellette, and sea salt. Cook on the grill until charred on all sides. Slice the Andouille and grill as well.

Spread some of the romesco on the bottom of the plate then drizzle some of the burnt olive oil on the plate. Toss the arugula with the reserved olives, Andouille, and octopus.

Noodle bars may be trending across the country, but pho and ramen joints are still few and far between in Connecticut. Thankfully, there are a few hidden gems serving the popular noodle soup across Fairfield County.

Serving classic Vietnamese dishes, including some of the best pho in Connecticut, is Bridgeport's Pho Mai. Fresh summer rolls, bahn mi and bubble tea are just a few of the traditional dishes on the menu. As its namesake suggests, it is Pho Mai's list of about twenty richly flavored Vietnamese soups, that makes this a must for noodle lovers.

Across town and firmly in the hole-in-the-wall category is Bridgeport's Pho Saigon. Inhabiting what feels like the living room of a small home, the menu (in both English and Vietnamese) offers a simple and inexpensive take on classic Vietnamese dishes.

Danbury's Pho Vietnam is a family-run BYOB restaurant opened by Tony Pham, occupying a tiny footprint in an unassuming strip mall. It has both the intimate feel and traditional flavors of a "mom-and-pop" restaurant, eschewing the trends of Asian fusion in favor of the type of home-cooked family dishes that owner Pham enjoys at home. "I want our community to experience Asian food the way it's supposed to be in a family setting. If I could merge food and family/friends together, it makes it worth it," says Pham.

Pham has recently expanded his Pho empire to the south with Mecha Noodle Bar in Fairfield. Embracing the ramen trend while still retaining his Vietnamese and Pho roots, Mecha's self-described "American-Vietnamese-Japanese-Thai-Chinese-Korean-inspired" menu casts a wider, more playful culinary net. Pho has a prominent place on the menu, and Pham's addition of ramen, and playful dishes such as his KFC Bao, a Korean-flavored fried chicken bun, allow him to span Asian culinary landscape.

Pho Mai
925 Wood Avenue, Bridgeport; (203) 916-7440

Pho Saigon
1275 Iranistan Avenue; Bridgeport; (203) 334-8812

Pho Vietnam
56 Padanaram Road, Danbury; (203) 743-6049; phovietnamrestaurant.com

Mecha Noodle Bar
1215 Post Road (US 1), Fairfield; (203) 292-8222; mechanoodlebar.com

SOUTHWEST CAFE

109 DANBURY ROAD
RIDGEFIELD, CT 06877
(203) 431-3398
SOUTHWESTCAFE.COM
OWNER: BARBARA NEVINS

Inspired by many years in New Mexico and a love for a cuisine largely defined by the chile pepper, Barbara Nevins opened Southwest Cafe in Ridgefield just over twenty-five years ago. Returning to the Northeast meant never quite shaking off the Southwest, and the cafe and its friendly community of regulars is a fitting homage to her past life in Taos.

Southwest Cafe's anchor is the chiles that are embedded throughout its menu. A nuanced vegetable in varying shades of green and red, chiles may be roasted, pickled, pureed, and dried, and these various iterations likely will find their way on Southwest Cafe's New Mexican menu. Nevins has cultivated a close relationship with a chile farmer just outside Hatch, New Mexico, and separately orders red chile power from Chimayó, New Mexico.

Each September during the crop's late summer harvest, nearly nine hundred pounds of chiles will arrive at the doorstep of Southwest Cafe, destined for any number of the restaurant's signature chile-laden dishes. This occasion is marked by an annual Hatch chile dinner, a tasting dinner made up five to eight courses that features the famously mild and subtle flavors of the chile.

Southwest Cafe is a fitting center point for Ridgefield's Marketplace, a small collection of artisan shops. Its relatively small space is made cozy by warm desert colors of dusty rose and yellow, with ristras and other southwestern adornments

hanging along the walls and the bar. At night, the crowd spills out onto a small patio illuminated by twinkling red plastic ristras and often punctuated by the sounds of live music.

The menu is broken up into small and big plates of classic New Mexican dishes such as Christmas chile rellenos, golden-brown batter-fried chiles filled with molten Jack cheese and nestled in both red and green chile sauces. The chicken borracho is a sweet and savory house specialty, a bone-in chicken served with a red chile and beer sauce, pickled tomatoes, and rice.

No Southwest meal is complete without tasting the chile stew—shards of slow-cooked chipotle pork swimming in a mixture of chiles and vegetables. The chipotle imparts a slow and smoky burn paired with the sweet green chiles, the perfect New Mexican comfort food dish.

Hatch Chile Stew

This very traditional Northern New Mexico staple is a favorite during chile harvest time.

(SERVES 6)

2 pounds pork stew meat, cut in cubes

1–2 tablespoons olive oil to brown the meat

2 large onions, peeled and chopped

3 (or more) cloves of garlic, chopped

2 cups chicken stock, or to cover

2 cups chopped roasted Hatch chiles, or as much as makes you happy

10 diced new potatoes

10 ripe plum tomatoes, chopped

Kernels from 1 ear of corn, preferably roasted on the grill

1 teaspoon dried Mexican oregano, or to taste

Grated cheese for serving

Flour tortillas for serving

Brown pork in olive oil. Remove from oil and set aside.

Add onions to the oil and cook until softened. Add garlic and cook about 3 minutes more. Add chicken stock, Hatch chiles, and pork. Simmer about 1 hour, partially covered.

Add the remaining ingredients (except cheese and tortillas) and simmer an additional hour.

Top with grated cheese and serve with warm flour tortillas.

Stanziato's Wood Fired Pizza

35 Lake Avenue Extension
Danbury, CT 06811
(203) 885-1057
STANZIATOS.COM
Chef/Owner: Matt Stanczak

An edgy take on Neapolitan-style pizza, Stanziato's Wood Fired Pizza in Danbury marries traditional style with modern flavors. Built on a satisfying trio of impeccable pizzas, seasonal salads, and craft beers, Stanziato's began as Danbury's best-kept secret and has emerged as one of the state's stand-out pizza destinations.

While traveling in Italy, the Culinary Institute of America–trained Matt Stanczak was struck by the beauty of Neapolitan pizza and its deceptively simple language of flour, water, and oil, paired with the rusticity of a wood fire and the time-honored rituals of preparation. Smitten by its tradition, the creative Stanczak interpreted the classic Neapolitan-style pizza and reinvented it by riffing on ingredient combinations, elevating the flavor and loft of its crust, and bringing it home by anchoring it with local produce from nearby Holbrook Farm.

Filled with local art, friendly service, and an outgoing chef, Stanziato's is a fun place to be. At the center of Stanziato's is an Italian-made wood-fired brick oven, powered by local hardwood that creates soaring temperatures approaching 800°F. This high heat allows the pizza to cook rapidly, producing Stanziato's signature crust—a pillowy cornichon (the Italian term for pizza's outer edge) dappled with char and a slightly tangy crust.

A menu of red and white pizzas takes center stage at Stanziato's with regular nightly specials, each a creative tour de force. Red pies are constructed around an uncooked San Marzano–based tomato sauce, from the red sauce and mozzarella of a Margherita to a woodsy cremini and caramelized-onion pie. The white pies tend to steal the show with their earthy combinations, such as a roasted cauliflower, burrata, and truffle oil, or a sopressata pizza that expertly balances the subtle heat of green chiles with the salty pork punch of Arthur Avenue sopressata. Beyond pizza is a list of flawlessly executed seasonal house-made salads and soups, wood-fired wings, and pastas. A changing menu of craft beers completes Stanziato's perfect circle of life.

The Diablo pizza is one of Stanczak's favorite white pies that can easily be made year-round.

Diablo Pizza & Cilantro Pesto

"The Diablo pie is a recipe that can easily be made year-round. A white pie brushed with gahhhlic/extra-virgin olive oil, sprinkled with a little sea salt or red pepper flakes, then topped with fresh mootz, butterflied shrimp butterflied, and finally, when it comes out of the oven, drizzled with the cilantro pesto, which really makes the pie pop."—Matt Stanczak

(SERVES 2)

For the cilantro pesto:

1 bunch cilantro, with stems
¼ bunch fresh parsley, with stems
¼ fennel bulb, plus some fronds, roughly chopped
2 limes, peeled, roughly chopped
4 ounces roasted nuts (almonds or hazelnuts)
1 cup olive oil
Kosher salt to taste
Cracked black pepper to taste

To make the pesto: Add all ingredients in food processor. Blend until it reaches a smooth consistency.

For the dough: "Use your favorite and simplest pizza dough recipe. The best are simply water, sea salt, fresh yeast, and flour."—Matt Stanczak

Toppings per pie:

Extra virgin olive oil to brush the dough
1 clove garlic
6 Maine shrimp or a Gulf shrimp, grilled and butterflied
3 ounces mozzarella, torn into bite-sized pieces
Pinch sea salt
Pinch red pepper flakes

Cilantro pesto (recipe above)
Cilantro leaves for garnish

Special equipment:

Pizza stone

To assemble: For each pizza, spread dough and brush the dough with extra virgin olive oil. Slice a clove of garlic paper thin and lay slices evenly on pie. Top with six shrimp and mozzarella. Sprinkle with sea salt and pinch of red pepper flakes. Place in your oven on a pizza stone or grill at 500°F or hotter for 5–10 minutes. Baking time will vary depending on your oven or grill. Once cooked, remove from the oven and finish with a drizzle of fresh cilantro pesto and garnish with a couple fresh cilantro leaves.

When it comes to pizza, Fairfield County owes a lot to its geography. Sandwiched in between the thin-crust style of New York and the coal-charred pies of New Haven, Connecticut's pizza joints tend to embrace both styles—with a deep appreciation for the mother of all pizza styles: Neapolitan. This is a region where big-name pizza chains need not apply.

In Stamford, a simmering rivalry between bar-style pizza purveyors Colony and newcomer Riko's is being waged over their nearly identical cracker-like crust. Their shared customer favorite is a hot oil pie, laden with hot peppers, or "stingers," and oil that has been steeped with hot peppers. (Colony Grill: 172 Myrtle Avenue, Stamford; colonygrill .com. Riko's Pizza: 170 Selleck Street and 581 Newfield Avenue, Stamford; ricospizzaonline.com)

In Greenwich, the ambitious ReNapoli (216 Sound Beach Avenue, Greenwich; renapoli.com) celebrates three distinct styles of Italian pizza making. A 900°F wood-fired oven creates Neapolitan pies, teglia pans are reserved for baking the loftier Romana-style pizza, and New York–style slices are available, fired in a 500°F gas-powered oven. Owner Bruno DiFabio has been making pizza for decades and has traveled extensively studying and perfecting his recipes and bringing them to bear on ReNapoli and his other pizza outposts in the region.

The most serious purveyors of Neapolitan-style are a trio of pizzerias that include Tarry Lodge Enoteca Pizzeria in Westport (page 166), Pizza Lauretano in Bethel (291 Greenwood Avenue; pizzerialauretano.com), and Stanziato's (page 152) in Danbury. They each begin with classic ingredients and technique informed by travels to the Napoli motherland, and an embrace of Caputo flour and wood-fired ovens, but each selectively interprets these elements, creating distinctive styles. New Haven–style pizza is strongly represented with Pepe's outposts in Danbury (59 Federal Road) and Fairfield (238 Commerce Drive; visit pepespizzeria.com for both). The original New Haven location was founded in 1925.

Strada 18

122 Washington Street
South Norwalk, CT 06854
(203) 853-4546
strada18.com
Owners: David Raymer, Steven Semaya, Luciano Ramirez,
and Henry Rosenblum

Hugging the western coast of Italy is a stretch of highway that pivots around Naples and extends to the very southern tip of the country. This road served as the initial inspiration for Strada 18, South Norwalk's artisanal Italian trattoria positioned along its own stretch of well-traveled road, Washington Street.

While traveling through Italy on his honeymoon, Chef David Raymer discovered an unassuming Italian truck stop with head-turning pizza. Once home, its vision haunted him as he cut his culinary path through kitchens from New York's Gotham Bar & Grill to Westport's Tavern on Main. Joining forces with his long-time sous chef Luciano Ramirez and cousin-in-law Steven Semaya, a former management consultant, they mined Raymer's wood-fired Italian vision to open Strada 18 in 2007.

Equal parts wine bar and pizzeria, Strada 18 is built around a menu of rustic Italian comfort food. Wood-fired pizzas and classic Italian trattoria dishes are joined by a formidable wine list of nearly four hundred (mostly Italian) bottles as well as a sizable beer menu. Strada's intimately narrow space is flanked by a pair of polished wooden bars. A wood-fired oven anchors the smaller bar, delivering pizzas and classic baked Italian dishes.

Red and white pizzas are topped with a variety of rustic Italian ingredients such as house-made sausage, duck confit, Sicilian anchovies, and white clam sauce, which benefit from the addition of house-made mozzarella. Beyond pizza, Strada's offerings skew classic trattoria with hearty baked pastas such as a signature veal Bolognese and oven-roasted specialties such as a chicken diavolo. At lunch, piadina (Italian flatbread sandwiches) and salads rule the daytime with Chef Raymer's cult favorite, a roasted salmon and brown rice salad.

BOULEVARD 18

A concept rooted in the classic French bistro model with a dash of gastropub, New Canaan's Boulevard 18 Bistro & Wine Bar (62 Main Street; boulevard18.com) is the Francophile sister concept to South Norwalk's Strada 18.

Boulevard 18 relies on a memorable burger, "snacks," and a thorough and worldly wine list.

POTATO-WRAPPED STRIPED BASS

(SERVES 4)

For the fish:

Salt and pepper to taste
2 (1½-pound) striped bass fillets
2 extra-large peeled Idaho potatoes
5 tablespoons butter, melted
2 tablespoons butter for the pan
2 tablespoons olive oil

For the bordelaise sauce:

1 cup red wine
1 tablespoon chopped shallot
1 cup veal stock
1 tablespoon heavy cream
4 tablespoons unsalted butter
Salt and pepper to taste

For the swiss chard:

2 bunches swiss chard
Salt
2 tablespoons unsalted butter
2 tablespoons olive oil
1 tablespoon chopped shallots
1 tablespoon chopped garlic
Salt and pepper to taste

Chopped tomato and chopped parsley for garnish (optional)

To prepare the fish: Lightly salt and pepper each fish fillet on both sides.

Using a mandoline or a slicer, slice the potatoes lengthwise, creating thin, long strips. Dip each slice in the melted butter and wrap it tightly around the fish, slightly overlapping them, until the whole fish is covered with potato slices. Refrigerate for at least 2 hours, until the potato/butter mixture firms up around the fish.

Preheat the oven to 350°F.

In an ovenproof sauté pan large enough to hold all four fillets comfortably, melt another 2 tablespoons butter in 2 tablespoons olive oil. Once melted, carefully place the fish in the pan and cook until nicely browned on one side; this should take about 4 minutes. Carefully turn the fish and place it in a 350°F oven. Cook for about 8 minutes, until just cooked through and nicely browned.

To make bordelaise sauce: Place the red wine and the shallot in a saucepan and reduce by one-third. Add the veal stock and reduce by half. Add the cream and bring the mixture back to a boil, and add cold pieces of butter. Add salt and pepper to taste.

To prepare the swiss chard: Thoroughly clean the swiss chard because it can be very sandy.

Blanch in salted water. Drain, cool, and squeeze dry. In a large sauté pan over medium-high heat, combine the butter and oil and heat until fairly hot and the foam from the butter subsides. Add the shallots and garlic, cook for 5 seconds and then add the chard, salt, and pepper. Cook until slightly wilted, about 4 minutes.

To serve: Place ¼ cup of cooked swiss chard on each plate. Place the fish carefully on top of the chard and nappe with the bordelaise sauce. If you like, garnish with chopped tomato and chopped parsley.

Veal Bolognese

(SERVES 2)

4 tablespoons butter
4 tablespoons olive oil
½ cup chopped carrot
½ cup chopped celery
½ cup chopped onion
2 cloves garlic
¼ cup finely diced guanciale or pancetta
1 pound ground veal
2 tablespoons tomato paste
½ cup half-and-half
1 (28-ounce) can San Marzano tomatoes
1 cup wine (any dry red or white or combo will do)
1 cup veal stock
Salt and pepper to taste

Place the butter and oil in a large saucepan over medium heat and heat until the butter has melted. Add the carrot, celery, and onion and cook until softened, about 10 minutes. Add the garlic and cook another 3 minutes. Add the guanciale and cook another 5 minutes.

Turn the heat to high and add the ground veal. Break up the meat with a spoon and cook until it loses its rawness. Add the tomato paste and cook for another 3 minutes. Add the half-and-half and cook until reduced and thickened. Add the tomatoes and wine and cook until reduced. Add the veal stock and simmer for about 1½ hours. Adjust the seasoning as needed with salt and pepper.

Serve over pasta.

PORRIDGE
CAKES

SUGAR & OLIVES

21½ LOIS STREET
NORWALK, CT 06851
(203) 454-3663
SUGARANDOLIVES.COM
OWNER/CHEF: JEN BALIN

Similar to each ingredient and every dish assembled at Norwalk's Sugar & Olives, the restaurant was conceived organically. Looking for a location for her popular kids' cooking classes, owner and chef Jen Balin found and transformed a formerly raw space in Norwalk into a buzzing commercial kitchen and cooking school in just under six weeks.

Balin didn't have a restaurant in mind, or even a formal menu in place for the first nine months her doors were open, as she focused solely on building a cooking school. A once-bare industrial factory space was made bright and happy by a palette of orange and gray walls, towers of well-worn cookbooks from her personal library, and communal seating. An open kitchen and prep space spans the width and nearly half the space, separated by a sleek white bar that doubles as the pass, giving way to a lofty succession of multiple seating areas. A comfortable lounge area, perfect for a lingering brunch crowd, and an adjacent dining room and communal table, a convivial hub for weekend dinners, soon turned Balin into an accidental restaurant owner and Sugar & Olives into a draw for eco-conscious diners.

Sugar & Olives's approach to food, like its wholesome namesake, is based upon simplicity and sustainability. Balin builds her recipes using quality, organic ingredients as building blocks, coupled with strictly sustainable restaurant practices. A regular of the Westport farmers' market, Balin uses her appearances as both a point of sale for her bottled dressings and prepared foods, and to network with the owners of Connecticut and nearby Hudson Valley farms, using them as ingredient sources for the restaurant and class menus. Many of the components and garnishes for each dish are made on-site when possible, including yogurt made from local milk, bread pudding made from their own freshly baked loaves, and even ketchup divined from in-season tomatoes. This mindful attention to ingredients, sources, and sustainable restaurant practices brings a clarity to each dish, and a three-star Green Restaurant certification speaks to this dedication.

Rolled eggs and a lobster lumberjack special rule a hearty and popular brunch menu, cheese plates and perfectly chopped salads characterize light lunches, and dinner plates that balance sweet and savory, such as sugarcane kebabs with salmon, speak to the elegant wholesomeness redolent throughout all of the Sugar & Olives menu.

No weekend is complete without a morning date with Sugar & Olives pancakes. Balin's aren't your ordinary pancakes. These skillet pancakes are topped with a bourbon-spiked whipped cream.

Chocolate Pancakes
with Bourbon Whipped Cream
(SERVES 6–8)

For the dry ingredients:

3 cups all-purpose flour
1 cup white whole wheat flour
1 cup cocoa powder
½ cup sugar
1 tablespoon plus 1 teaspoon baking powder
1½ teaspoons salt

For the wet ingredients:

6 eggs
2 cups whole milk
1 cup buttermilk
½ cup sour cream
½ cup canola oil
¼ cup best-quality grade B maple syrup

For the bourbon whipped cream:

1–2 tablespoons bourbon, or to taste
1 cup whipped cream
Confectioners' sugar for garnish

To make the pancakes: Whisk together all the dry ingredients in a large bowl and then run it through a sifter. Set aside.

Combine all the wet ingredients in a blender and pulse for two 5-second intervals.

Pour the wet into the dry ingredients and mix well. Transfer this gorgeous batter into a pitcher and chill overnight; a pretty batter needs a night's rest.

Preheat oven to 350°F.

Heat up a 6-inch ovenproof skillet (NOT a nonstick skillet) for 3 minutes, then remove it from the heat and spray it with cooking spray. Return to the heat for another minute, pour in some batter (enough to fill up the pan's diameter less than halfway), let it sit on a medium heat for 2 minutes.

Transfer the pan into the preheated oven and bake for 12–15 minutes. Using a pot holder, remove the pan and, using a metal spatula, flip over your prize. Return to the oven and continue to bake for 5–6 minutes or until firm and puffy.

To make bourbon whipped cream: Combine whipped cream with bourbon.

To serve: Plate pancakes and sprinkle with confectioners' sugar and a dollop of bourbon whipped cream.

Tarry Lodge Enoteca Pizzeria

30 Charles Street
Westport, CT 06880
(203) 571-1038
tarrylodge.com/westport
Owners: Mario Batali, Joseph Bastianich, Andy Nusser,
and Nancy Selzer
Executive Chef: Mario LaPosta

With one foot planted in Connecticut, perfecting Tarry Lodge's pizzas, and the other in his family's hometown just north of Naples, Executive Chef Mario LaPosta's devotion to pizza is undeniable.

You could say that pizza runs in LaPosta's blood. Throughout his life, annual trips to Italy and generations of family pizzerias stoked a nearly life-long obsession with pizza. As soon as LaPosta graduated from college, he headed for Italy, determined to learn the traditions of pizza making as close to the source as possible. He spent that summer working in successive stages, first in Rome and then in Naples, at some of its most revered outposts, such as Pizzeria Brandi, the birthplace of the Margherita. These traditional proprietors didn't teach recipes or specify technique but instilled a deep respect for the history and importance of pizza as cultural heritage.

Upon LaPosta's return to the United States, he soon found himself with an offer to join the opening team of Tarry Lodge in Port Chester, New York, an Italian trattoria concept owned by the Batali & Bastianich Hospitality Group. LaPosta was hired as pizzaiolo at the new restaurant and spent his first few years perfecting its pizza before running the kitchen under the tutelage of Andy Nusser. He was soon tapped to return to his home state of Connecticut to open Tarry Lodge's second location in the burgeoning Saugatuck neighborhood of Westport.

It was during a time of focused pizza research at Tarry Lodge that LaPosta's prowess with the Margherita pizza would place him tenth in the world at the pizza-making championships in Italy. As executive chef and pizzaiolo at Tarry Lodge Enoteca Pizzeria, LaPosta governs not only its kitchen but also its commanding steel-clad eighty-two-

inch Mugnaini oven. The big and beamy wood-fired oven is surrounded by a wraparound marble bar—prime seats to watch the near-constant pizza action by the Tarry Lodge team.

Tarry Lodge's pizza style is chiefly Neapolitan, a thin yet chewy, charred pizza made outstanding with an array of earthy Italian combinations, from the popular Margherita, to stand-out combinations such as a guanciale, black truffle, and sunny-side up egg; burrata with pancetta and chili oil; and potato, leek, rosemary, and lardo.

Each of Tarry Lodge's pies begin with dough—a combination of salt, fresh yeast, "00" flour, and water—followed by a six-hour direct rise. The sauce is a simple combination of good-quality imported tomatoes, and most pies are anchored with house-made mozzarella from Grande curd. The oven operates at 900°F, which means pies take between sixty and ninety seconds to cook, ensuring a signature char but leaving very little room for error.

The rest of the menu is classic trattoria with antipasti, insalate, secondi centered around seared proteins, and a greatest hits of popular Batali pastas such as a Bolognese tagliatelle. As the word *enoteca* (literally translated as wine repository) in its title connotes, the wine list is a diverse list of Italian wines representing nearly all of the country's regions.

Since opening, Tarry Lodge has become a bit more seasonally focused, seeking inspiration from the Westport farmers' market and weekly deliveries from Sport Hill Farm.

Pizza Margherita

(MAKES TWO 12-INCH PIZZAS)

For the pizza dough:

¼ ounce fresh yeast

2 cups room-temperature water

1⅓ pounds "00" flour (recommended), or
    unbleached all-purpose flour, divided

1 ounce sea salt

For the pizza:

1 teaspoon sea salt

5 ounces crushed San Marzano tomatoes

6 ounces fresh mozzarella, small dice preferred

6 basil leaves

2 tablespoons olive oil

Special equipment:

Standing mixer with dough hook

Pizza stone

Rolling pin (optional)

Pizza peel

To make the pizza dough: Dissolve fresh yeast in room-temperature water and place in a standing mixer fitted with a dough hook. Begin mixing and gently add half the flour over 2 minutes. Add the salt, then add the remaining flour over 3 minutes, and knead for 1 minute more in mixer.

Remove dough, divide into two parts, roll each half into a ball, cover, and set aside. Let dough rise for 3–4 hours.

To make the pizza: Preheat the pizza stone in a 450°F oven for 30 minutes.

Once dough has risen, dust each half with flour and begin pressing it flat with your fingers; if you want a thick, puffy crust, don't press the crust. Finish stretching the dough by hand or with a rolling pin until the dough is a 12-inch round. Dust the pizza peel lightly with flour and place one dough round on the peel.

Add the salt to the crushed tomatoes and evenly spread over dough, leaving the outer ½ inch around for the crust. Sprinkle with mozzarella and basil, and drizzle with olive oil. Slide off the peel onto the hot, preheated stone. Bake for 8–12 minutes, until pizza is just crisp and golden brown.

Buon appetito!

Terrain Garden Café

561 Post Road East
Westport, CT 06880
(203) 226-2750
shopterrain.com/westport-restaurant
Chef: Joe Wolfson

Terrain Garden Café blends seamlessly into its large retail home—an airy and inspired mecca for high-end home and garden style. The lines between retail and restaurant are purposefully blurred, down to the cafe's gardener-inspired details: A small clay pot functions as a warm and encompassing bread plate, Ball jars serve as water glasses, a tree sprouts from the middle of the dining room, and the menu's trowel and spade motif artfully echo dining utensils.

Blending southern style and French techniques, Chef Joseph Wolfson's approach is suited to Terrain's practiced and refined rusticity. Local and seasonally peak-perfect ingredients make this menu hum alongside carefully sourced protein. Ham, in all its glorious iterations, figures prominently on this southern-slanted menu. "I'm a southern boy, so I love pork. We make our own bacon, serve pork belly at brunch, and often have pork shoulder or a chop on the menu," says Wolfson when asked of his preferred protein.

Wolfson's French-southern mix is evident across brunch, lunch, and dinner. From a house-made lamb merguez with oyster mushroom and Parisian gnocchi to fried green tomatoes with sweet pepper chowchow, Wolfson breathes new (southern) life into seasonal cooking, hinting at the complexity that often emerges from the kitchen.

Born in Texas and raised in South Carolina, Wolfson credits his mother and grandmother, excellent home cooks who served as his culinary guideposts, as the inspiration to pursue a culinary education at Johnson & Wales in Charleston. Following school, Wolfson pursued successive posts inside some of the South's most prominent kitchens, including The Ocean Room, a five-star restaurant and resort on South Carolina's Kiawah Island and Alabama's Ham & High, known for its fully sustainable kitchen.

Westport's Terrain is a perfect home for the transplanted chef, where its diners often seek out exceptional seasonal ingredients and the uniquely southern style Chef Wolfson brings to the hybrid restaurant and retail space.

Buttermilk Fried Chicken
& Apple Corn-Bread Waffles

(SERVES 4)

For the chicken:

2 teaspoons paprika

2 teaspoons cayenne pepper

2 cups buttermilk

1 whole chicken cut into an 8 pieces (2 breasts, 2 legs, 2 thighs, 2 wings)

3 cups all-purpose flour

1 teaspoon garlic powder

1 teaspoon onion powder

2 tablespoons salt

1 tablespoon coarse ground black pepper

1 gallon canola oil

Salt and pepper to taste

For the waffle batter:

4 tablespoons butter

3 Granny Smith apples, peeled and cut into medium dice

¾ cup packed light brown sugar

6 large room-temperature eggs, separated

¾ cup granulated sugar

1 cup milk

1 cup buttermilk

2 cups all-purpose flour

1½ cups cornmeal

1 teaspoon baking soda

Hot sauce (such as Sriracha) for serving

To prepare the chicken: Whisk 1 teaspoon paprika and 1 teaspoon cayenne into the buttermilk, then add the chicken. Allow to marinate, covered, in the refrigerator at least 4 hours but up to 1 day.

Mix all the dry ingredients, including the remaining paprika and cayenne, together. Drain the chicken, then dredge the chicken in the dry ingredients.

Heat the oil to 350°F in a large skillet or pot. The depth of the oil should reach about halfway up the largest piece of chicken.

Very gently drop the chicken into the hot oil, making sure to avoid splashing it on yourself. Adjust the temperature to ensure that it stays at a constant 350°F. Cook until the chicken pieces reach an internal temperature of 160°F, and then drain them on paper towels and season with salt and pepper.

To make the waffles: In a sauté pan melt the butter, then add the apples and brown sugar. Cook over medium heat until the apples are soft and well glazed.

In a stand mixer whip the egg whites until they reach a hard peak, remove and reserve.

In a clean bowl, whip the egg yolks and the granulated sugar in the stand mixer, and slowly pour in the milks until they are well incorporated. Add in the dry ingredients and whip them until smooth. Fold in the apples and egg whites by hand with a rubber spatula, making sure not to overwork them.

When the batter is ready, pour it into a properly greased waffle iron and cook until golden brown.

To serve: Plate the chicken and waffles together with maple syrup and your favorite hot sauce; Chef Wolfson recommends Sriracha.

THALI

296 Ethan Allen Highway, Ridgefield, CT 06877
87 Main Street, New Canaan, CT 06840
4 Orange Street, New Haven, CT 06510
THALI.COM
CHEF/OWNER: PRASAD CHIRNOMULA

With five restaurants in three Connecticut towns, Prasad Chirnomula has largely defined Indian cuisine for much of the state. Mining the traditional and regionally diverse dishes of India, Thali's contemporary interpretation of its cuisine has become the restaurant's signature concept.

Each dish is a reflection of the years Chirnomula spent in his native India, as well as his frequent trips back to the country on what he calls his "spice journeys." As a result, many dishes are culinary postcards that speak to the beloved regions and rituals of a diverse country and its equally diverse cuisine.

The Konkan crab, a jumbo lump blue crab with a silky coconut-, ginger-, and mustard-infused sauce recalls the western state of Goa. A traditional dosa, a rice and lentil crepe-like bread common in southern India, is served with four of Thali's signature chutneys, including a coconut, onion, cilantro, and lentil version. Central to each entree is a bowl of fragrant basmati, a fluffy rice with toasted spices.

Chirnomula's charisma and energy is deeply embedded in both the dishes of his restaurants as well as its bold interiors. From his first outpost in New Canaan in a former bank, to Ridgefield and New Haven, saturated primary colors and bold textures set the tone for each restaurant. Chirnomula takes as much pride in designing the menus as he does selecting paint color for each of his restaurants.

Born and raised in India, Chirnomula emigrated to Connecticut in 1985 after attending the Food Craft Institute of Poona and becoming the director of Food & Beverage at the Ritz in Hyderabad, India. He has slowly built his Thali empire, recently broadening his culinary reach with Oaxaca Kitchen, a Mexican fusion restaurant in New Haven. In addition to running his six restaurants, Chef Chirnomula leads annual tasting tours of India and is a frequent host of cooking classes.

SEASIDE MOILEE

(SERVES 4–6)

Choice of seafood (3 pounds total):

Mussels

Clams

Shrimp

Scallops

1 large Spanish onion

2 green serrano chiles

1-inch ginger piece

2 tablespoons canola oil

½ teaspoon black mustard seeds

8 curry leaves

½ teaspoon turmeric

Salt to taste

32 ounces coconut milk, preferably Chaokoh brand
(available through patelbrothersusa.com/newsite)

3 teaspoons lemon juice

Steamed basmati rice for serving

Clean and prep your choice of seafood. Peel and finely chop the onion. Slit the green chiles into long slices and remove the seeds. Peel and grate the ginger.

Heat the oil in sauté pan, add mustard seeds, and when they splatter, add curry leaves, onion, long slit green chiles, and grated ginger, and cook until soft and translucent, about 5 minutes. Add turmeric and salt, and sauté for 1 minute. Add coconut milk and bring to boil. Now add the seafood and cook for 5 minutes or until the seafood is done. Add 3 teaspoons lemon juice and stir and serve with steamed rice.

BOONDI AVOCADO CHAT

Boondi is a Rajasthani snack food made from sweetened, fried chickpea flour. *Chat* or *chaats* are savory snacks often found on the streets of India and Pakistan.

(SERVES 4)

For the guacamole:

2 ripe avocados
1 small red onion, peeled and minced (about ½ cup)
2 tablespoons finely chopped cilantro leaves
1 teaspoon fresh lime juice, or to taste
Coarse salt to taste
½ jalapeño chile, stem and seeds removed, chopped into small dice
1 ripe tomato, seeds and pulp removed, chopped

For the boondi chat:

2 cups Surati Boondi*
½ cup minced tomato
½ cup minced purple onion
¼ cup chopped cilantro
¼ cup minced mint
¼ teaspoon MDH Chunky Chat Masala*
2 tablespoons Swad Mint Chutney*
¼ cup Swad Tamarind Chutney *
*Available through patelbrothersusa.com/newsite.

Thin slices of red radishes, chopped tomatoes, and chopped fresh cilantro for garnish
½ teaspoon finely minced roasted garlic (optional)

To make the guacamole: Cut avocados in half and remove the seeds. Scoop out the avocado from the peel and put it in a mixing bowl.

Using a wooden ladle or spoon, mash the avocado. (Remember to leave it a bit chunky and fully mashed) Add the chopped onion, garlic, cilantro, lime, and salt and mash some more.

Chile peppers vary in their hotness, so, start with half of one chile pepper and add more if desired.

Add the chopped tomato to the guacamole and mix well.

To make the boondi chat: In a large bowl, gently mix together the ingredients just before assembling the chat.

To serve: Layer the guacamole and the boondi chat and garnish with radishes and some more chopped tomatoes and cilantro.

Valencia Luncheria

164 Main Street
Norwalk, CT 06851
(203) 846-8009
VALENCIALUNCHERIA.COM
Chef/Co-Owner: Michael Young
Co-Owner: Luis Chavez

The *arepa* is a fried or pan-roasted handmade corn cake filled with a nearly endless variety of ingredients. At Valencia, this traditional Venezuelan food and its endless iterations serve as the foundation for what is Norwalk's most unpretentious and popular restaurant.

Beginning as a tiny eight-table luncheonette, Valencia Luncheria has evolved into something of an elder statesman for Fairfield County's dining scene. First opened in 2008 as a BYOB restaurant, Valencia drew a rabid following that was drawn to its self-described Venezuelan beach food and reasonable prices. In 2012 it reopened a few doors down with triple the space, a liquor license, and an expanded menu.

The culinary soul of Valencia can best be defined as Latin American comfort food: *Arepas,* empanadas, and burritos, offered alongside black beans, rice, and plantains, form much of its foundation. These staples may be ubiquitous in the bodegas of cities such as Norwalk, Stamford, and Danbury, but none of them can claim Chef Michael Young in their kitchens.

Young grew up in New York, influenced by his French chef father who first ignited his passion for cooking. Spending time in various kitchens, it was the nuevo latino style of Chef Douglas Rodriguez that galvanized what would become his signature blended-Latin approach. In Connecticut, Young made his way through former Norwalk hot spots Habana and Ocean Drive before settling down and opening Valencia with partner Luis Chavez.

Downshifting expectations of the typical white-tablecloth restaurant without sacrificing quality, Valencia fuses nuevo latino food with the casual style of a neighborhood "*luncheria*," drawing regulars from every walk of life as well as a cameo on *Diners, Drive-ins and Dives.* The duo's sphere of influence continues to grow, with sister restaurant concept Bodega Taco Bar (page 126) in nearby Fairfield and Darien.

At breakfast and lunch, Valencia's nearly thirty *arepas* are something of a naturally occurring phenomenon, from the Aphrodite (mango and avocado) to Ruby (plaintain, *queso blanco*), with empanadas and burritos figuring prominently as well. Dinner shifts toward heartier and traditional Venezuelan fare with *platos tipicos de Venezuela* and *platos fuertes* represented in equal parts seafood and meat, with the requisite rice and beans by their side.

Young's ribs are legendary at both Valencia and Bodega. A frequent special on the Valencia menu, these ribs are a deeply earthy and richly spiced dish.

CHOCOLATE-CHILE BABY BACK RIBS

(SERVES 2)

For the ribs:

3 tablespoons New Mexican chile powder

1 tablespoon dark brown sugar

½ teaspoon onion powder

½ teaspoon ground cumin

½ teaspoon garlic powder

1 rack pork baby back ribs, usually 14 bones

2 cups water

1 can cola, preferably Coca-Cola

For the chocolate-chile sauce:

4 tablespoons diced white onion

1 medium tomato, chopped

3 tablespoons olive oil

2 chipotle chiles packed in adobo sauce

4 ounces Mexican chocolate

2 ounces panela (unrefined whole cane sugar)

Salt and pepper to taste

Sliced green onions for garnish

Procedure for the ribs, to be done one day in advance: Preheat the oven to 375°F. Mix all dry seasonings and coat the rack of ribs with them. Pour water and cola in a roasting pan. Place the ribs in pan, with cut side of ribs facing down. Cover roasting pan and bake for 90 minutes. Remove ribs, and let rest until cool. Refrigerate overnight.

To make the sauce: Sauté onions and tomato in olive oil for 7 minutes. Add chipotle, chocolate, and panela and simmer for 10 minutes over low heat. Let cool and then puree. Add salt and pepper to taste.

To assemble: Cut rack of ribs into separate pieces. Reheat them in a sauté pan with the chocolate-chile sauce for 8 minutes. Garnish with sliced scallions.

SAUGATUCK CRAFT BUTCHERY

An old-fashioned butcher shop with modern-day ideals, Saugatuck Craft Butchery (580 Riverside Avenue, West-port; craftbutchery.com) celebrates the skills and traditions of butchering a unique selection of pasture-raised meats from small, sustainable farms. They source whole animals that have been humanely raised; they are one of the few butchers in the country to source and butcher following a nose-to-tail philosophy, using every part of the animal.

Saugatuck Craft Butchery is the result of the convergence of owner Ryan Fibiger's keen knife and business skills. Once a Wall Street investment banker, Fibiger left banking to attend Fleisher's Grass Fed and Organic Meats' whole animal butchery program in Kingston, New York. He is a constant and knowledgeable presence at the shop, and a frequent collaborator with chefs and farmers around the region. The name Saugatuck Craft Butchery has become synonymous with quality among discerning restaurant owners across Fairfield and New Haven. Fibiger also hosts special events and popular classes such as "Butchering 101."

CARLO AREPA

(SERVES 4)

For the chicken filling:

1 (3½-pound) whole chicken
1 large white onion, julienned
4 cloves garlic, chopped
1 poblano pepper, julienned
1 red pepper, julienned
4 tablespoons olive oil
1 (28-ounce) can whole plum tomatoes, crushed by
    hand
2 tablespoons hot sauce
2 tablespoons Worcestershire sauce
1 tablespoon oregano
¼ cup chopped fresh cilantro
Salt and pepper to taste

For the arepa dough:

2½ cups warm water
1 teaspoon salt
1 tablespoon fennel seeds
3 tablespoons brown sugar
2 cups white corn flour, preferably Harina Pan
1 tablespoon olive oil
Additional oil for cooking the arepas

For the stuffing:

1 avocado, sliced
1 cup shredded queso blanco

To make the chicken: Place the whole chicken in a soup pot, cover with lukewarm water, and boil on low until chicken is completely cooked. Remove chicken, allow chicken to cool, and pull meat off of bones. Discard bones and skin.

In separate sauté pan, sauté onions, garlic, poblano peppers, and red peppers in olive oil until softened. Add plum tomatoes, hot sauce, and Worcestershire sauce. Cook on low for 30 minutes. Incorporate chicken but do not overstir. Toss in the chopped cilantro, oregano, and salt and pepper to taste.

To make arepa dough: In mixing bowl, add warm water, salt, oil, fennel seeds, and brown sugar. Slowly incorporate the corn flour, while mixing by hand; if the flour is added too quickly, the dough will be lumpy. Mix until the flour is incorporated. It will resemble very smooth, wet dough. Cover and let rest for 10 minutes.

Preheat the oven to 400°F.

Form the dough into 5-ounce patties. (This will make about 8 arepas, depending on size.) Make sure that edges of each patty are smooth and free of cracks. Coat the skillet with olive oil, and heat it over medium heat. Cook the arepas 5 minutes on each side, then place them on a baking sheet and cook in a 400°F oven for 5 minutes.

To serve: Slice each arepa halfway through and pinch the sides to create an opening. Stuff with chicken, avocado, and cheese, and serve.

THE WHELK

575 RIVERSIDE AVENUE
WESTPORT, CT 06880
(203) 557-0902
THEWHELKWESTPORT.COM
OWNER/CHEF: BILL TAIBE
OWNER/SOMMELIER: MASSIMO TULLIO

Fresh, sustainable seafood on the Saugatuck River—The Whelk presents one of Connecticut's most creative and sophisticated seafood menus. Led by Chef Bill Taibe and Sommelier Massimo Tullio, there is little pretense behind this exceptional Westport oyster bar.

The Whelk's menu—from raw bar offerings to its larger plates—is a delicious illustration of and education on the bounty of Connecticut fishermen. Shifting daily based

on availability, The Whelk's offerings kick off with impeccably fresh bivalves figuring prominently in a variety of preparations, from raw to barbecued and fried. Periwinkles, whelks, and shad roe are usually rare sights on menus, but in season they appear frequently at The Whelk.

From the simple and raw—freshly shucked oysters served with Taibe's jalapeño-spiked mignonette—to the more layered and nuanced, such as a warm mélange of an addictive smoked-trout dip served with house-made Parker House rolls, the menu encourages sharing. Arranged in sizes and often delivered to the table in waves, The Whelk's menu ignores categorical convention and tends toward grazing. The proximity of Saugatuck Craft Butchery (page 180) ensures its meat is meticulously sourced, from a lamb burger to the chef's southern-inspired fried chicken sandwich with pimento cheese and pickles.

The Whelk's interior reflects the clean, whitewashed look and understated tones of a seafaring weekend in Maine with a hipster edge—bead-board paneling, warm wood, and nautical touches, paired with white subway tiles, park bench–inspired seating, and a prominent white marble bar lined with industrial metal stools.

The two men behind The Whelk are no strangers to the Fairfield County dining scene. Gregarious chef and owner Bill Taibe is a James Beard award–nominated chef also behind leFarm (page 102), known for creative, farm-centric cuisine. Co-owner and sommelier Massimo Tullio is a consistent and reassuring presence in the dining room, and the expert and guide on the restaurant's evolving wine list, helping diners select perfect pairings for any meal. He may be most familiar from his seven years at Norwalk's Fat Cat Pie Company (page 88).

Both dishes shared by Taibe feature a glimmer of his love for pork: shrimp and grits with Tennessee country ham and seared scallops with bacon.

SHRIMP & GRITS WITH JALAPEÑO BUTTER & TENNESSEE COUNTRY HAM

(SERVES 2–4)

For the grits:

5 cups milk
1 cup stone-ground grits (preferably from Anson Mills)
Salt and pepper to taste

For blackening seasoning:

1 tablespoon Old Bay Seasoning
1 tablespoon cayenne pepper
1 tablespoon crushed red pepper
1 teaspoon black pepper
1 teaspoon mustard seed
1 teaspoon fennel seed
1 teaspoon smoked paprika
1 teaspoon Aleppo pepper
½ teaspoon coriander
½ teaspoon cumin

For jalapeño butter:

1 shallot, peeled and sliced
2 thyme sprigs
1 teaspoon whole black peppercorns
1 cup white verjus
1 cup white wine
1 cup butter, cut in small cubes
1 pickled jalapeño, diced small

For the shrimp:

12–16 shrimp
salt to taste
prepared blackening seasoning to taste
grapeseed oil for pan

1 slice Tennessee country ham cut into 2 x 2-inch pieces

To make the grits: Bring the milk to a boil in a large saucepan and add grits. Whisk for 10 minutes. Lower heat to low and continue to cook until grits are cooked through (time depends on the grind). Season with salt and pepper.

To make the blackening seasoning: Mix all ingredients and grind in a coffee grinder.

To make the jalapeño butter: Place shallot, thyme, black peppercorns, verjus, and white wine in a saucepan and reduce to 2 tablespoons. Add butter, a couple of cubes at a time, to emulsify the butter slowly into the reduction. Strain and add diced jalapeños.

To make the shrimp: Season shrimp with salt and blackening seasoning. Coat bottom of saute pan with grapeseed oil. Heat up pan over high heat

and when hot, sear shrimp on all sides. Then add enough jalapeño butter to cover the shrimp, plus a little more. Turn burner to low/medium heat and let shrimp cook in butter until done.

To serve: Place a spoonful of grits in each bowl. Place 3 to 4 pieces of shrimp on grits with a little jalapeño butter from pan. Lay a piece of ham over each shrimp. Sprinkle blackening spices over each dish.

Seared Scallops with Farro, Corn, Beans & Bacon

(SERVES 2–4)

For the farro:

4 cups water
2 cups farro
Salt and pepper to taste

For the vegetable ragout:

2 tablespoons unsalted butter
2 slices bacon, cooked until crispy and cut in small
   pieces
2 ears corn, charred on a grill and cut from the cob
2 cups fresh green pole beans, blanched in boiling
   water and shocked in ice water

For the scallops:

1 tablespoon canola oil
8 (U-10) or 12 (U-20) scallops
Salt and pepper to taste
2 tablespoons unsalted butter
1 thyme sprig

To make the farro: Bring water to a boil and add farro. Cover and remove from heat. Let it sit covered for 30 minutes. Stir and add salt and pepper to taste.

To prepare ragout: Heat butter in a sauté pan. Add all the ingredients and heat through.

To prepare the scallops: Heat canola oil in a sauté pan. Season scallops with salt and pepper and add to pan. Cook until scallops are a medium brown color, about 2 minutes over medium heat. Add butter and thyme and flip scallops. Cook another minute or so, basting the scallops with the hot butter and thyme.

To serve: Place 2 or 3 scallops on a bed of farro on each plate. Garnish with vegetable ragout.

Index

About the Author

Amy Kundrat is the executive editor of CTbites, the award-winning website devoted to chronicling great food in Connecticut, especially her home in Fairfield County. A communications specialist with a concentration in new media, Amy's career leading external communications teams has taken her from world-class art museums to technology start-ups, and academic institutions. She currently works in New Haven at Yale University, where she indulges in the city's vibrant food-truck scene. She lives in the woods of northern Fairfield County with her husband.

About the Photographer

Stephanie Webster is the editor in chief and founder of CTbites.com. Born and raised in New York City by parents who design restaurants for a living, she developed a passion for finding out-of-the-way gems during weekly trips to the depths of Chinatown and frequent trips abroad. Professionally she began her career as a photo editor in the magazine industry and then migrated to the world of new media consulting and website building during New York's first dot-com wave. She led strategy, brand development, site architecture, and content development assignments for top consumer brands. A seven-year excursion to Seattle exposed her to a casual yet innovative approach to food that hadn't yet made it to the East Coast. When she relocated back to Connecticut, she made it her quest to find great food and support a community of eaters that live for their next meal.